Letts
Framework FOCUS

Different cultures and traditions

Nick Jones

Contents

Authors & contexts | Activities and English Framework Teaching Objectives

YEAR 7

1 Greetings!
Poems
- Benjamin Zephaniah (England) — A Reading & Speaking: W22 SL17 — 4
- James Berry (Caribbean) — B Creative Writing: W22 SL16 — 7
- Jackie Kay (Scotland) — C Reading & Discussion: R7 SL12 — 7

2 Who are you?
Poems
- Abdourahman Waberi (N Africa) — A Reading & Discussion: R8 R19 SL14 — 10
- Benjamin Zephaniah (England) — B Reading & Discussion: R7 R14 R19 — 12
- Trad. Ewe (West Africa) — C Creative Writing: WR9 — 14
- D Discussion: SL12 — 14

3 Talking stories
Folk stories
- Trad. Ashanti (West Africa) — A Speaking: SL2 — 16
- Grace Hallworth (Caribbean) — B Reading & Speaking: R6 WR5 SL17 — 17
- C Reading & Writing: R12 R15 WR7 — 20

4 An Arabian Night
Story & Playscript
- Trad. Arabian — A Critical Reading: S18 R14 WR7 — 22
- Dominic Cooke (England) — B Writing & Drama: S15 R18 WR9 SL16 — 25

5 On reflection
Paintings & Poems
- Edward Hopper (USA) — A Reading Images: R8 R12 SL12 — 28
- Julie O'Callaghan (USA / Ireland) — B Reading Images: R8 R12 SL12 — 30
- Sujata Bhatt (India) — C Creative Writing: WR7 WR8 — 32

YEAR 8

6 Do as I say
Playscript & Story
- Ken Campbell (England) — A Reading & Drama: R5 SL15 — 33
- Jamaica Kincaid (Caribbean) — B Critical Reading & Writing: R11 R16 WR18 — 35

7 First to speak
Stories & Ballad
- Trad. Maharashtra (India) — A Reading to compare: R8 R11 R16 — 38
- Trad. Scottish — B Writing or Speaking: WR9 SL2 — 41
- Trad. Northern English — C Reading & Speaking: S11 R11 SL16 — 41

8 Animal magic
Poems & Painting
- Norman Silver (South Africa) — A Critical Reading: W11 R7 R10 — 43
- Trad. Malagasy (Africa) — B Critical Reading: W11 R14 — 45
- Gillian Clarke (Wales) — C Creative Writing: WR6 WR9 SL10 — 49
- José Garcia Cordero (Caribbean)

9 Colour
Poems
- Helen Dunmore (England) — A Critical Reading: W11 R10 SL10 — 50
- Grace Nichols (Caribbean) — B Reading & Creative Writing: R7 R16 WR7 — 53
- Benjamin Zephaniah (England) — C Critical Reading: W13 R16 — 56
- John Agard (Caribbean) — D Critical Writing: R11 WR18 — 58

10 Money
Playscripts
- Anon. Middle English — A Reading for Meaning: S13 R10 — 59
- Obotunde Ijimere (West Africa) — B Reading & Discussion: R10 R16 — 61
- C Creative Writing & Performance R16 WR9 SL16 — 68

YEAR 9

	Authors & contexts	Activities and English Framework Teaching Objectives	
11 I remember Stories & Poem	Margaret Atwood (Canada)	**A** Creative Writing: R11 WR5	69
	Jean Rhys (Caribbean)	**B** Critical Reading & Writing: R6 R10 WR17	72
	Susan Marie Scavo (USA)	**C** Reading & Speaking: R10 SL13	74
		D Creative Writing: WR6	76
12 Migration Poems	Gillian Clarke (Wales)	**A** Reading & Speaking: R7 SL9	77
	James Berry (Caribbean)	**B** Speaking & Creative Writing: WR8 SL13	80
	Grace Nichols (Caribbean)	**C** Reading for Meaning: R16	82
	Jean Binta Breeze (Caribbean)		
	Imtiaz Dharker (Pakistan)		
13 Weird tales Stories & playscript	Trad. Hausa (West Africa)	**A** Reading & Discussion: R6	86
	Trad. Fipa (East Africa)	**B** Reading & Drama: R10 SL12	89
		C Creative Writing: WR5 SL12	91
14 The one Poems, Playscript & Painting	Alice Walker (USA)	**A** Reading & Discussion: W7 SL9	93
	Dudley Randall (USA)	**B** Reading for Meaning: R6 R14 SL13	95
	Trad. Rwanda (E Africa)	**C** Reading & Creative Writing: R10 R16 WR8	98
	Tanika Gupta (India)		
	Gustav Klimt (Austria)		
	Lawrence Ferlinghetti (USA)		
15 Man Friday Novel & Playscript	Daniel Defoe (England)	**A** Creative Reading: R6 R15 WR17	102
	Adrian Mitchell (England)	**B** Drama & Reading: R6 R14 R16 SL14	105
		C Critical Writing: R9 R16 WR16 WR17	110

Key to English Framework Teaching Objectives

W = Word level   R = Reading   SL = Speaking and Listening   S = Sentence Level   WR = Writing

YEAR 7 UNIT 1

Greetings!

Aims

In this unit, we'll look at some poems that include languages and dialects other than standard English, and at the relationship between language and accent. We'll also reflect on the experience of moving from one form of language to another.

Starter session

How many ways are there to say 'hello' and 'goodbye'?

Starting from one corner of the room, each student in turn greets or says farewell to the next student – but each time using a different word or phrase. Speak loudly. Choose words from other languages if you like. Can you get around the whole class?

A READING AND SPEAKING

1 Take a look at Text 1 – Benjamin Zephaniah's poem '**Greet Tings**'. It's a poem that contains a number of different languages, but – as you'll discover – it doesn't need translating…

- As a class, how many different languages can you recognise?

- Now try reading the poem aloud a couple of times, either around the class or in groups. Don't worry if the words you're reading look unfamiliar. Just pronounce them as you think they might be pronounced, in a loud voice. Remember – it's a greeting!

- One of the things you may have discovered is that Zephaniah is playing with language, as poets so often enjoy doing. *Some* of these greetings can be found in dictionaries from around the world (different *languages*). Others are written-down versions of things English speakers say when they meet each other (different *dialects*). Which do you think are which?

- The poem's title also plays with language. What has the poet done here?

TEXT 1

Greet Tings

Assalaam Alaikum
Hola
Szia
Sat Srii Akaal
Wa Happen
Zdravo
Yia Sou
Merhaba
Hej
Yo
Sawast Dee Craap
Ciao
Zdraustvuyte
Endemenesh
Ahoj
Bonjour
Yassou
Shalom
Namaste
Dag
Guten Tag
Buenos Dias
Parev
Ehida
Selamat Datong
Dia Dhuit
Hallo
And Welcome

Benjamin Zephaniah

Context

Benjamin Zephaniah is one of Britain's best-known poets. He writes and performs poems both for adults and young people, and his work is available both in books and on CDs. Born in Birmingham, he grew up in Jamaica and in Handsworth, and many of his poems are written in Caribbean English dialect. *Talking Turkey*, from which '**Greet Tings**' comes, has been one of the most popular books of poems for young people in recent years.

2 Now read Text 2 – James Berry's '**Bye Now**', written in what is sometimes called 'nation language', an Afro-Caribbean version of English.

- Even though it may look unfamiliar, try reading this poem aloud to each other in pairs. See if you can find an accent that fits the dialect, and decide what the lines mean.

When James Berry published this poem, he added a second version – '**Goodbye Now**' (Text 3) – that converts the Caribbean dialect into Standard English. For example, the first line substitutes 'well' for 'good', because in Standard English 'good' is not used as an adverb. (If there were lines in the first version that you couldn't work out, this translation should help to sort things out.)

3 Read this second version – '**Goodbye Now**' – aloud. Does it come across in the same way? Which version do you prefer?

TEXT 2

Bye Now

    Walk good
        Walk good
Noh mek macca go juk yu
Or cow go buck yu.
Noh mek dog bite yu
Or hungry go ketch yu, yah!

Noh mek sunhot turn yu dry.
Noh mek rain soak yu.
Noh mek tief tief yu
Or stone go buck yu foot, yah!
    Walk good
        Walk good

James Berry

TEXT 3

Goodbye Now

    Walk well
        Walk well
Don't let thorns run in you
Or let a cow butt you.
Don't let a dog bite you
Or hunger catch you, hear!

Don't let sun's heat turn you dry.
Don't let rain soak you.
Don't let a thief rob you
Or a stone bump your foot, hear!
    Walk well
        Walk well

James Berry

Context

James Berry is another poet who has lived both in the West Indies and in the United Kingdom. Born in 1924, he grew up in Jamaica, and moved to Britain shortly after the Second World War, a time when immigration was particularly encouraged. He has written several popular books for younger readers, including *When I Dance* (from which the poem '**Bye Now**' is taken) and *A Thief in the Village* (a set of stories), as well as some fine poetry for adult readers.

B CREATIVE WRITING

We'll now use '**Greet Tings**' (Text 1) and '**Bye Now**' (Text 2) as models to create something similar. Benjamin Zephaniah's poem uses single words or very short phrases, while James Berry develops the ideas into slightly longer sentences, but the basic form is much the same: each line is a way of saying 'hello' or 'goodbye' to someone.

1 Work in small groups – or as a whole class if your teacher prefers. Write a poem in two sections, the first containing different ways of saying 'hello', and the second different ways of saying 'goodbye'.

- Some of these words or phrases may be borrowed from languages other than English – how many languages do you possess between you as a class?
- Some of your chosen phrases may be to do with different styles of talking. Do you say different things to different friends?
- Think also about differences between generations. For example, my grandfather used to say 'So long' when we parted, while my daughters say 'Speak-to-you-soon.'
- Remember to experiment – like Benjamin Zephaniah – with different ways of writing things down.

C READING AND DISCUSSION

1 Listen to your teacher read Text 4 – Jackie Kay's poem '**Old Tongue**', and start to consider what the poem is saying about language and what it means to us.

- Some of the Scottish words that the poet uses have descended from the language of Gaelic. Over time, English has gradually replaced Gaelic as the language of Scotland. Others are versions of English words, based on differences of accent, i.e. the way words are pronounced. Saying these words aloud may help you to guess their meaning. What might an 'Eedyit' be, for example?
- One of the things Jackie Kay refers to is the difference in the pronunciation of 'scone'. The dictionary tells us that the word originated in Scotland, and means 'a small, flat, circular, baked, dough-cake.' The dictionary also notes that there are different ways of pronouncing the word.

- If you yourself use the word 'scone', do you say something that rhymes with 'stone', or something that rhymes with 'John'? It's not just a case of England saying it one way, and Scotland another — I grew up in Gloucestershire, and we used to called them 'scons'. (The 'e' at the end may seem to suggest the 'stone' version, but there's also the word 'gone'… .)
- The last few lines of '**Old Tongue**' focus on the poet's feelings about moving from one way of speaking to another: 'Did you ever feel sad when you lost a word?', she asks us.

2 As a class, talk about the language experiences you yourselves have had.
- Some of you may have learned English as an additional language.
- Some of you may have begun with English, then added an additional language.
- Some of you, like Jackie Kay, may feel they have started to lose touch with a language or a dialect that they no longer speak or hear as much as they used to.

3 Talk also about *accents*, and what they mean to us.
- Have you ever have moved into an area where the language was the same, but the accent different?
- Do you know people whose voices change when they telephone old friends or relatives?
- Are there TV dramas where the way people talk makes a particular impression on you?
- Have you ever wanted to change the way you talk?

Review

This unit has looked at language differences, and what they mean to us. The poems we have read have featured a range of *languages*, *dialects* and *accents*.
- As a class, discuss what these poems have made you think about your own language or languages, about the ways in which you talk, and about the language of other people that you know.
- Listen to a reading aloud of one of the poems created in Activity B.

TEXT 4

OLD TONGUE

When I was eight, I was forced south.
Not long after, when I opened
My mouth, a strange thing happened.
I lost my Scottish accent,
Words fell off my tongue.
Eedyit, dreich, wabbit, crabbit
Stummer, teuchter, heidbanger,
So you are, so am ur, see you, see ma ma,
Shut yer geggie or I'll gie you the malkie!

My own vowels started to stretch like my bones
and I turned my back on Scotland.
Words disappeared in the dead of night,
new words marched in; ghastly, awful,
quite dreadful, *scones* said like *stones*.
Pokey hats into ice cream cones,
Oh where did all my words go —
my old words, my lost words?
Did you ever feel sad when you lost a word,
did you ever try and call it back
like calling in the sea.
If I could have found my words wandering,
I swear I would have taken them in,
swallowed them whole, knocked them back.

Out in the English soil, my old words
buried themselves. It made my mother's blood boil.
I cried one day with the wrong sound in my mouth.
I wanted them back; I wanted my old accent back,
my old tongue. My dour, soor Scottish tongue.
Sing-songy, I wanted to *gie it laldie*.

Jackie Kay

Context

Jackie Kay, as the poem mentions, spent the first eight years of her life in Scotland, before moving to north-west England. As well as poetry and a novel for adult readers she has written three books of poems for younger readers – *Two's Company, Three Has Gone*, and *The Frog Who Dreamed She Was an Opera Singer* – which are well worth looking out for.

Vocabulary

dreich: *boring*
wabbit: *worn out*
stummer: *fool, dud, failure*
laldie: *thrashing*
teuchter: *word used by Scots Lowlanders to refer to Scots Highlanders.*

YEAR 7 UNIT 2

Who are you?

Aims

In this unit, we'll look at two poems that reflect on the idea of identity. We'll also explore the way the poems are written, and link this to some personal writing of your own.

Starter session

On a slip of paper, complete the following statements:

- My name is…
- I am…
- I am not a…
- Sometimes I…

Then hand your slip to your teacher, who will read some of them aloud, but without saying the name of the author. Can you guess who has written each list?

A READING AND DISCUSSION

1 As a class, talk about what the word 'identity' can mean.
   - Have you ever filled in a form, for example, in which you are asked to provide some basic information about who you are – your surname, for instance. What other basic *facts* might such forms ask for?
   - Now think of the kind of questions which people get asked when they are interviewed in a magazine – questions like: 'What is your favourite…?' These questions, too, are about identity, though in a different way. They are to do with people's *opinions* – what matters to them, how they see things.

2 Here is a little questionnaire – though the questions aren't necessarily the ones you might expect.
   - Working individually, jot down a word or a phrase to complete each of these sentences:
     – My name is…
     – My tree is…
     – My river is…
     – My book is….
     – My main endeavour is to…
     – My dream is to…

- Now invent 3 more statements of this kind, starting 'My [something] is…', and add them to your list.
- Then compare your list with someone else's. How does your identity come across?

3 Now listen to a reading of **'Nomadic Poem'** (Text 1), by Abdourahman Waberi. Then in pairs or small groups read the poem again and discuss what you think it means.
- What comes over most strongly about the identity of the speaker in this poem?
- How is this identity different from your own? Look again at the lists each person has written, and what they suggest.

Context

Abdourahman Waberi

The writer of this poem is from Djibouti, on the north-east African coast. The poem's speaker is telling us what it is like to live as a nomad in the desert regions of North Africa or Arabia. The speaker seems to belong to a certain kind of landscape, rather than a town or even a country. The poem has been translated into English by Véronique Tadjo.

TEXT 1

NOMADIC POEM

my tree the aloe plant
my flower the crack in the cactus
my river there is none in my country
my basaltic universe in the desert
my close circle of camels
my weapon the dagger
my shadow is lanky
survival is my main
endeavour
my scenery the unchanging horizon
the dust stirred up by my soles of sheep's hide
the territory always
in front of me
my guide the desert
my book the sky
every evening picked up
my speech each stone
each flint
my dream always the same:
the nomadic child
in the simplest state of being

Abdourahman Waberi

Vocabulary

nomadic: travelling. A 'nomad' is someone who moves from place to place, particularly across desert landscapes, in search of water and pasture
aloe: a spikey, herbal plant, found in desert regions
basaltic: rocky, made of basalt

B READING AND DISCUSSION

The second poem in this unit (Text 2) focuses on one aspect of identity – where someone has come from. Listen to a reading of Benjamin Zephaniah's **'The British'**.

One of the things that might strike you about this poem is the *form* in which it is written. You'll probably have come across writing of this sort before, though perhaps not in a poem.

1 In pairs, jot down a list of any words or phrases in the poem that remind you of recipe language. For example, how many *instructional verbs* can you see?

2 What does the phrase 'melting pot' mean to you? If you put things 'in a melting pot', what are you hoping will happen?

3 Britain's population (and the English language) has always been a mixture of 'ingredients'. As a class, check if you know the whereabouts of each of the countries mentioned in the poem.

The last few lines of the poem – including the 'Note' and the 'Warning' – focus on the idea that led the poet to want to write it. (Poems often end this way.)

4 What does Benjamin Zephaniah want to say about *national identity*?

5 And why do you think he chose to write this poem in recipe form?

Vocabulary

The poem records the various 'ingredients' which have gone to make up the British population:

The *Celts* were early (Stone Age) inhabitants of Britain. When their country was invaded, first by *Romans* and then by *Anglo-Saxons*, the Celts were driven into the far corners – Cornwall, Wales, Ireland, Scotland.
At around the same time, the *Picts* lived in Scotland, and the *Silures* in Wales.

The *Romans* invaded Britain in first century AD, and left in the fifth century. After that, the kingdom was invaded by *Angles*, *Saxons* and *Jutes* (from what is now Germany), and by *Vikings* (from Denmark and Norway). The *Normans* arrived from France in 1066, and dominated England for some time.

Most of the other nationalities mentioned in Zephaniah's poem began to arrive in the eighteenth and nineteenth centuries, as global contact expanded, then increasingly in the twentieth century. *Bajans* are from Barbados (West Indies).

TEXT 2

THE BRITISH
Serves 60 million

Take some Picts, Celts and Silures
And let them settle,
Then overrun them with Roman conquerors.

Remove the Romans after approximately four hundred years
Add lots of Norman French to some
Angles, Saxons, Jutes and Vikings, then stir vigorously.

Mix some hot Chileans, cool Jamaicans, Dominicans,
Trinidadians and Bajans with some Ethiopians,
Chinese, Vietnamese and Sudanese.

Then take a blend of Somalians, Sri Lankans, Nigerians
And Pakistanis,
Combine with some Guyanese
And turn up the heat.

Sprinkle some fresh Indians, Malaysians, Bosnians,
Iraqis and Bangladeshis together with some
Afghans, Spanish, Turkish, Kurdish, Japanese
And Palestinians
Then add to the melting pot.

Leave the ingredients to simmer.

As they mix and blend allow their languages to flourish
Binding them together with English.

Allow time to be cool.

Add some unity, understanding and respect for the future
Serve with justice
And enjoy.

Note: All the ingredients are equally important. Treating one ingredient better than another will leave a bitter, unpleasant taste.

Warning: An unequal spread of justice will damage the people and cause pain. Give justice and equality to all.

Benjamin Zephaniah

> **Context**
>
> **Benjamin Zephaniah**
>
> See *p.5*. **'The British'** comes from Zephaniah's book *Wicked World*, which explores international experience in a lively and thought-provoking way.

C CREATIVE WRITING

This task asks you to think about yourself, and the things that make you who you are – your personal identity. Choose either of the following (or both, if you have time).

1 Write an identity poem using **'Nomadic Poem'** (Text 1) as a model.
   - The notes you made during Activity A might provide some ideas.
   - Start with some lines which follow the basic pattern of Abdourahman Waberi's poem:
     'My _____ is _____'.
   - Then, like Abdourahman Waberi, vary the sentence construction as you write. For example, some of the lines could start 'When I…', or 'If I…'
   - But each line should reveal something about who you are, and what you are like.

Or:

2 Write a recipe poem that tells someone how to create a version of you.
   - You'll need to decide on a food metaphor. Are you fried, curried, baked? Half-baked? Are you a cold dish? You could give yourself a meal name: Ben Pizza, Amy Massala…
   - Recipes often start with a list of ingredients, and this might be a good way to plan your poem. What flavours should they add, for example? You could then include this list in the final version if you wish.
   - Follow the patterns of recipe language. You could use **'The British'** (Text 2) as a model – or use a recipe book.
   - When the recipe is finished, you might like to add a 'Note', or a 'Warning', as Benjamin Zephaniah does at the end of his poem. What will your maker need to be careful about?

D DISCUSSION

1 The traditional African poem, **'A Baby is a European'** (Text 3), says a number of things about babies. What does it suggest about the way Africans have viewed Europeans over the years?

TEXT 3

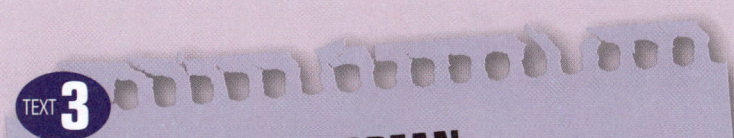

A BABY IS A EUROPEAN

A baby is a European
he does not eat our food:
he drinks from his own water-pot.

A baby is a European
he does not speak our tongue:
he is cross when the mother understands him not.

A baby is a European
he cares very little for others:
he forces his will upon his parents.

A baby is a European
he is always very sensitive:
the slightest scratch on his skin results in an ulcer.

Traditional: Ewe (West Africa)

Context

This is a written English translation of an oral poem spoken by a member of the Ewe tribe, from Togo, in West Africa. West Africa was where the European slave trade began in the seventeenth and eighteenth centuries, and was later colonised by a range of European nations – Britain, France, Spain, Portugal, The Netherlands.

Review

This unit has explored the concept of *identity* – how we think of ourselves, how other people think of us, how we think of other people. We have also looked at – and experimented with – different *poetic forms*.

- As a class, talk about the differences, as you see them, between *personal* identity and *national* identity. Which matters to you most? And why is that?
- Listen to a reading aloud of one of the poems created during Activity C.

YEAR 7 UNIT 3

Talking stories

Aims

This unit focuses on traditional storytelling, and on the relationship between speech and writing. We'll experiment with both telling and writing stories, and take a look at story structure.

Starter session

Do a 'Chinese Whisper' around the class. Your teacher will give one student a sentence to whisper to the next, and so on – and a different sentence to another student at the other end of the room. Try and pass on the exact words, and the way they are spoken. What has happened to the sentences by the time they have been whispered all the way around the class?

A SPEAKING

Here is a 'skeleton' version of a traditional tale that has been told across many cultures, from India through to England.

i A bearded traveller is staying at an inn. He asks to be woken early.
ii As he sleeps, a joker shave off his beard.
iii The traveller is woken late, and leaves in a hurry.
iv On the way, he discovers he has no beard.
v He hurries back the inn, and explains they have woken the wrong man.

1 Now do this in pairs. Close your copy of this book, and retell the story to each other in turn – then re-open the book…

Not too difficult? You now have the skeleton of the story in your heads, and can start to flesh it out a bit. It will still be a short tale, but the five points could perhaps develop into five spoken paragraphs, building towards the final punch line.

- You could perhaps mention how or why things happen.
- And think about the style you tell the story in. Will you start, for instance, with:

> There was once a traveller…

or with

> There was this bloke, right, …

2 Working together, devise your own version of the story, and tell it to another pair.

B READING AND SPEAKING

All the stories in this unit come from *oral traditions*. For many years, people have told these stories to each other – enjoyed them, memorised them, passed them on. No one knows who first invented them, or when. Each time the stories are told, some of the details may change, but the *skeleton* remains the same. Eventually, versions of these stories may get written down by someone who has heard them.

The second story – **'Talk'** (Text 1) – is more complicated. Begin by listening to it read aloud.

Oral storytellers don't need to memorise the exact words, but they do need to memorise the order in which things happen. That's why most oral stories have a clear pattern, often with repetitions.

1 Working in pairs or small groups, work out a plan for telling a version of this story. You can shorten it a bit if you like. The plan needs to fit on one side of a sheet of paper. For example, it could start:

　i　Once – Accra – Farmer – digging
　　Yam says
　　Dog says
　　Tree says
　　Farmer runs away

　ii　Farmer meets Fisherman… etc

Then use the plan to practise your version of the story. Divide the telling between you, so no-one has too much to do.

2 When the rehearsals are completed, listen to a couple of groups telling their version of the story.

TEXT 1

TALK

Once, not far from the city of Accra on the Gulf of Guinea, a country man went out to his garden to dig up some yams to take to market. While he was digging, one of the yams said to him:

'Well, at last you're here. You never weeded me, but now you come around with your digging stick. Go away and leave me alone!'

The farmer turned around and looked at his cow in amazement. The cow was chewing her cud and looking at him.

'Did you say something?' he asked.

The cow kept on chewing and said nothing, but the man's dog spoke up.

'It wasn't the cow who spoke to you,' the dog said. 'It was the yam. The yam says leave him alone.'

The man became angry because his dog had never talked before, and besides, he didn't like his tone. So he took his knife and cut a branch from a palm tree to whip his dog. Just then the palm tree said:

'Put that branch down!'

The man was getting very upset about the way things were going, and he started to throw the palm branch away, but the palm branch said:

'Man, put me down softly!'

He put the branch down gently on a stone, and the stone said:

'Hey, take that thing off me.'

This was enough, and the frightened farmer started to run for his village. On the way he met a fisherman going the other way with a fish trap on his head.

'What's the hurry?' the fisherman asked.

'My yam said, "Leave me alone!" Then the dog said, "Listen to what the yam says!" When I went to whip the dog with a palm branch the tree said, "Put that branch down!" Then the palm branch said, "Do it softly!" Then the stone said, "Take that thing off me!"'

'Is that all?' the man with the fish trap asked. 'Is that so frightening?'

'Well,' the man's fish trap said, 'did he take it off the stone?'

'Wah!' the fisherman shouted. He threw the fish trap on the ground and began to run with the farmer, and on the trail they met a weaver with a bundle of cloth on his head.

'Where are you going in such a rush?' he asked them.

'My yam said. "Leave me alone?"' the farmer said. 'The dog said "Listen to what the yam says!" The tree said, "Put that branch down!" The branch said, "Do it softly." And the stone said, "Take that thing off me!"'

'And then,' the fisherman continued, 'the fish trap said, "Did he take it off?"'

'That's nothing to get excited about,' the weaver said, 'no reason at all.'

'Oh yes it is,' his bundle of cloth said. 'If it happened to you you'd run too!'

'Wah!' the weaver shouted. He threw his bundle on the trail and started running with the other men. They came panting to the ford in the river and found a man bathing.

'Are you chasing a gazelle?' he asked them.

The first man said breathlessly:

'My yam talked to me, and it said, "Leave me alone!" And my dog said, "Listen to your yam!" And when I cut myself a branch the tree said, "Put that branch down!" And the branch said, "Do it softly!" And the stone said, "Take that thing off me!" '

The fisherman panted:

'And my trap said, "Did he?" '

The weaver wheezed:

'And my bundle of cloth said, "You'd run too!" '

'Is that why you're running?' the man in the river asked.

'Well, wouldn't you run if you were in their position?' the river said.

The man jumped out of the water and began to run with the others. They ran down the main street of the village to the house of the chief. The chief's servants brought his stool out, and he came and sat on it to listen to their complaints. The men began to recite their troubles.

'I went out to my garden to dig yams,' the farmer said, waving his arms. 'Then everything began to talk! My yam said "Leave me alone!" My dog said, "Pay attention to your yam!" The tree said, "Put that branch down!" The branch said, "Do it softly!" And the stone said, "Take it off me!"'

'And my fish trap said, "Well, did he take if off?" ' the fisherman said.

'And my cloth said, "You'd run too!"' the weaver said.

'And the river said the same,' the bather said hoarsely, his eyes bulging.

The chief listened to them patiently, but he couldn't refrain from scowling.

'Now this really is a wild story,' he said at last. 'You'd better all go back to your work before I punish you for disturbing the peace.'

So the men went away, and the chief shook his head and mumbled to himself, 'Nonsense like that upsets the community.'

'Fantastic, isn't it?' his stool said, 'Imagine a talking yam!'

Traditional: Ashanti (West Africa)

Vocabulary

yam: a tropical root vegetable, like a potato

Context

This story comes from the Ashanti people, whose homeland is Ghana in West Africa. This English translation is from a book called *African Voices*, edited by Peggy Rutherford. The city of Accra is the capital of Ghana, and the Gulf of Guinea is a name given to the West African ocean.

C READING AND WRITING

1 Read Grace Hallworth's **'The Shiner'** (Text 2), based on a Caribbean legend – the text printed here contains most of the story, but not the ending.

- At what point in the story did you begin to sense that the policeman might be in danger? Were there details that made you think 'Uh-oh…' ?

The section of Grace Hallworth's book in which this story appears is headed 'La Diablesse', the name given to the Caribbean she-devil about whom many stories are told. (The she-devil has a French name because French is the standard language of several West Indian islands.)

Here are some known facts about La Diablesse, based on various Caribbean folk-tales:

- She only appears at night.
- She can take on different forms.
- She keeps her face concealed.
- She tries to lure people into lonely places.
- Two things repel her: smoke, and the sight of a crucifix.
- The thing that destroys her is salt.

2 With this information in mind, how do you think the story might continue?

- What kind of dangers might the policeman be about to face?
- Does the policeman survive unharmed – or not?
- What will he have to do to survive?
- Remember that the story is called **'The Shiner'** – does that give you any ideas?

Your task is to finish writing the story, in no more than 300 words.

Review

This unit has looked at *oral tradition*, and at the process of telling and re-telling stories. We have looked at the *skeletons* on which oral stories are based, and how *endings* are set up.

- How many students in your class have themselves learned stories from oral tradition – for example, from relatives at family gatherings? Can you remember them? Have you ever re-told any? Would you like to?
- Listen to a reading aloud of one of the stories created during Activity B.

TEXT 2

THE SHINER (extract)

Late one night a policeman was riding home when he saw a young woman walking along a road. The policeman was young and eager for a bit of excitement. He was also a new recruit and did not have the experience which encourages caution, so he approached the woman.

'A young lady like you should not be out alone at this hour,' he said.

The woman appeared to be shy for she kept her face hidden and did not reply.

The policeman persisted. 'Would you like a lift home on my bicycle?' he asked.

The woman continued walking and said nothing. Her attitude made him more determined.

'Come now, lady,' he urged. 'Surely you don't believe I would harm you. Just tell me where you live and I will see you home safely.'

The woman stopped and shyly said, 'It's not far from here but if you insist I will go with you.'

She was hoisted on the crossbar and they set off pleasantly enough. The policeman was teasing and joking, and though the woman was laughing merrily she hardly said a word. They had not gone very far when the policeman found that he could not turn the pedals as easily as before, yet the road was quite flat. He thought to himself, 'She was as light as a bundle of feathers when we started off. Now she is a dead weight.' He began to feel uneasy as he remembered he had not seen her face.

'Lady, you didn't tell me where you live,' he said.

'Just a little way to go. Keep straight on,' she replied with a strange laugh.

After a few seconds passed with no more directions, he asked, 'Lady, how much further?' Her reply was the same as before, 'Just a little way to go. Keep straight on.'

The policeman was labouring with the load he carried. He felt as though his lungs were bursting and fear seeped through every pore of his skin as he recalled that there were no houses ahead of them. He was heading for a part of the town where the only buildings were warehouses. Beyond them lay the open sea…

Grace Hallworth

Context

Grace Hallworth

Grace Hallworth was born in Trinidad, later moving to England where she worked as a librarian. She has always had a strong interest in traditional Caribbean stories and legends. She performs these stories herself, and has published a collection of written-down versions called *Mouth Open Story Jump Out* (Methuen), where the full text of 'The Shiner' appears.

As published here the story is incomplete (see Activity C).

YEAR 7 UNIT 4

An Arabian Night

Aims

In this unit we'll look at a traditional tale from the classic collection *The Arabian Nights*, and a recent dramatisation of it. We will investigate storytelling styles and techniques of dramatic adaptation.

Starter session

Your teacher will write an interesting sentence from a story on the board. You should suggest ways in which the sentence could be spoken aloud by the whole class. How could it be divided up? Which bits could be spoken by a single voice, and which by several? Which might be louder, which quieter? Try out some possibilities.

A CRITICAL READING

Listen to your teacher read the story of **'The Historic Fart'** (Text 1), then look at what the note says about the context of this tale. The story itself is around 800 years old, and this written English version comes from the 1920s, so some of the language may be unfamiliar. Check the Vocabulary box for any words that need explaining.

What we're going to focus on is the story's *narrative structure* – how it is shaped and organised. In one way the narrative is quite simple, because it's mainly about a single character. So most of the sentences have his name, Abu al-Hasan (or his pronoun, 'Abu'), as their subject. But let's look at how the story works its way from beginning to end.

Discuss these questions as a class or in groups.

1 The story is divided into six paragraphs. Can you decide why the writer ends and begins each paragraph where he does?

2 What period of time does each paragraph cover?

3 What is the *mood* of each paragraph? How is Abu feeling? How is the reader feeling? Is there a word in the paragraph which sums up the mood?

4 The third paragraph seems to be a key paragraph in this story. How might you read this paragraph aloud?

5 One way of describing narrative structures goes like this:

introduction > *development* > *crisis* > *resolution*.

Do these labels match any of the paragraphs you have been looking at? Are there other labels you could use?

TEXT 1

THE HISTORIC FART

It is related that there was once in the city of Kaukaban, in Yemen, a man whose name was Abu al-Hasan. At an early age he left nomadic life and had become a polished citizen and rich merchant. He had married in his youth, but Allah had called his wife into His mercy after a year of marriage; thus it was that Abu al-Hasan's friends were always pressing him to marry again.

At length Abu al-Hasan could hold out against these persuasions no longer; so he entered into communication with the old women who negotiate marriages, and became betrothed to a damsel as beautiful as the moon shining on the sea. He gave great feasts to celebrate the wedding and asked not only friends, but also the fakirs and dervishes of the city. He opened wide the doors of his house and provided for his guests rice of seven different colours, sherberts, lamb stuffed with nuts, almonds, pistachios and raisins, and a young camel roasted and presented whole. All the guests ate and drank joyfully, and when the bride had been shown seven times, dressed in different and costly robes, she was led round for an eighth circle, so that those eyes might gaze their fill which were not yet satisfied. After that the old women led her into the bridal chamber and, upon a bed as high as a throne, prepared her in every way for the entrance of her lord.

Abu al-Hasan came slowly and with dignified step into the chamber, and sat for a moment on the divan to prove, both to himself and to his wife and the women, that he was a man of gravity and good manners. He rose weightily to receive the wishes of the old women and to dismiss them, before going up to the bed where the girl so modestly awaited him; but, ah, horror, his belly was full of heavy meat and drink! He let out a fine, terrible, resounding fart! May the Devil be far from us! Each old woman turned to her neighbour and began speaking in a loud voice, pretending that she had heard nothing; the bride, instead of laughing or mocking, chinked and rattled her bracelets to add to the covering noise. But Abu al-Hasan, more than half-dead with mortification, pleaded a pressing need and ran down into the court. He saddled his mare and, leaping upon her back, fled through the shadows of the night away from his house, his marriage, and his bride. He left the city, he crossed the desert, he came to the sea side and went aboard a boat bound for India. In time he came to the Malabar coast.

There he became acquainted with many men from Yemen, who spoke so well of him to the King of that land that he was appointed captain of the royal guard. He lived in enjoyment of that post for ten years, honoured and respected in the midst of luxury; and whenever the memory of his fart came to him, he banished it from his mind as an unclean thing.

But at the end of those ten years he was seized with a great longing for his native land and pined for his city and his house, and well-nigh died of his exile. One day he could resist the wishes of his soul no longer; therefore, without even asking leave of the King, he slipped away and returned to Yemen. He disguised himself as a dervish and, journeying on foot towards Kaukaban, came to a hill which overlooked that city. He gazed down upon the terrace of his old house and, with tears in his eyes, exclaimed: 'Pray God that no one recognises me! May He have made them forget!' He came down from the hill and took side-streets that would lead him to his house. As he went he saw an old woman sitting at her door, taking the lice from the head of a little ten-year-old girl. He heard the child saying: 'Mother, I wish to know my age; one of my friends is going to cast my horoscope. Tell me when I was born.' The old woman reflected for a moment, and then said: 'You were born on the night and in the year when Abu al-Hasan let his fart.'

The unhappy Abu al-Hasan turned and fled, giving his legs to the wind. 'Your fart has become a date!' he lamented. 'It will go down in history, as long as there are palm trees.' And he did not cease his flight till he was back in India, where he lived in the bitterness of exile until his death. Allah pity him!

Traditional: Arabia. Translated by Powys Mathers

Context

The Arabian Nights is a magnificent collection of stories originating from the Arab world in around the thirteenth century – though many of the stories had been circulating orally, in India, Persia and Arabia, for centuries before that. Holding them all together is the story of Shahrazade, a young woman who marries a King who has been betrayed by a previous wife's unfaithfulness. In revenge, the embittered King has vowed to execute each of his wives after a single night. But by telling him a story each night, and then offering to tell him another, Shahrazade persuades him to postpone the execution for a thousand and one nights, by which time he has been so well entertained that he gives up the idea of executing her altogether. He then discovers that she has by this stage borne him three children.

'The Historic Fart' is the story Shahrazade tells on night No. 616. This literary translation, by Powys Mathers, was written in the 1920s.

Vocabulary

nomadic: travelling
Allah: Islamic God
betrothed: engaged to be married
damsel: old English word for young unmarried woman (cf French 'mademoiselle')
fakirs and *dervishes*: Muslims who devote themselves to a life of religious poverty
pistachio: type of nut
gravity: seriousness
divan: seat, sofa (an Arab word which has now been adopted into English)
modestly: shyly, innocently
mortification: distress
pine for: long for something you have lost
well-nigh: nearly
exile: living abroad (when you'd prefer to live at home)
lament: cry out in sadness or despair

B WRITING AND DRAMA

'The Historic Fart' was one of the stories included in the Young Vic Theatre's dramatisation of *The Arabian Nights*.

1 Do a class reading aloud of the extract from **'How Abu Hassan Broke Wind'** (Text 2) printed below, which covers the first half of the story, and needs a cast of twelve. (The part of the Fart could perhaps be played by the whole class!)

2 As a class, talk about the style of this dramatisation, aimed at a contemporary audience, including young people. Do you think the story would come across any differently in this form?

3 Then, in pairs, write a script which adapts the second half of **'The Historic Fart'**. You could either continue in the style of the Young Vic version, or use a different style if you prefer.

HOW ABU HASSAN BROKE WIND (extract)

SHAHRAZADE:	It is said that in the city of Kaukaban in Yemen there was a man who was the wealthiest of merchants called Abu Hassan. His wife had died when she was very young and his friends were always pressing him to marry again.
ABU HASSAN:	So, weary of being nagged, Abu Hassan approached an old woman…
MARRIAGE BROKER:	…a marriage-broker…
WIFE:	…who found him a wife with eyes as dark as a desert night and a face as fresh as the dawn.
ABU HASSAN:	He arranged a sumptuous wedding banquet and invited …
UNCLE AND AUNT:	…uncles and aunts …
PREACHER AND FAKIR:	… preachers and fakirs …
FRIEND AND FOE:	… friends and foes …
GREAT AND GOOD:	… and the great and the good from all around.
ALL:	The whole house was thrown open for feasting.
UNCLE AND AUNT:	There was rice of five colours …
PREACHER:	… sherbets of many more …
FRIEND:	… goats stuffed with walnuts…
FOE:	…and almonds and pistachios …
GREAT AND GOOD:	… and a whole roast camel …
ALL:	So they ate and drank and made merry …
WIFE:	… and the bride was displayed, as is the custom, in her seven dresses to the women …
WOMEN:	… who couldn't take their eyes off her.
ABU HASSAN:	At last, the bridegroom was summoned to go up to his wife …
WIFE:	…who sat on a golden throne …
ABU HASSAN:	… and he rose with stately dignity from the sofa. When all of a sudden he let fly a huge and deafening fart…
	We hear a deafening fart.
AUNT:	Immediately each guest turned to his neighbour …
FAKIR:	… and busied himself in pressing conversation as if his life depended on it.
ABU HASSAN:	But a fire of shame was lit in Abu Hassan's heart. So he excused himself and instead of going to his wife, went down to the stables, saddled his horse and rode off weeping bitter tears through the blackness of the night …

Adapted by Dominic Cooke

Context

In 1998 the Young Vic Theatre presented a dramatised version of the *The Arabian Nights* (or some of them…) as a Christmas show, adapted and directed by Dominic Cooke. A cast of nine performers played all the roles between them, accompanied by musicians.

Review

This unit has looked at how a traditional oral story can be adapted into different *literary forms*: in this case a *prose* version, and a *dramatisation*. We have looked in particular at *narrative structure*, and how writers create *mood*.

- As a class, talk about any differences you have noticed between the forms of prose narrative and dramatisation, and how they work? What is the strength of each form?
- Listen to a reading aloud of one of the playscripts created during Activity B.

YEAR 7 UNIT 5

On reflection

Aims

In this unit, we'll look at how people interpret pictures, and how paintings can become a starting point for poems and stories. We'll think about character, setting and mood, both in pictures and in writing.

Starter session

Your teacher will point to a series of colours around the classroom. You could then suggest what each colour might be called if it were a new brand of paint. Use hyphens: *shark-fin blue* etc. Try and make the names as eye-catching as possible. Collect ideas on the board. How does the mind convert colours into words?

A READING IMAGES

1 As a class, take a look at Edward Hopper's picture **'Automat'** (Picture 1), painted in 1927. (In those days the word 'automat' referred to a café with self-service slot machines.)

- How would you describe the *mood* of this picture? What do you guess the woman might be thinking about?
- There's a huge window behind her, but we can't see anything through it. How does that affect the atmosphere of this picture? (Would it be different if we could see a city street, for example?)
- What does the empty chair make you think?

2 Now read the poem 'Automat' by Julie O'Callaghan (Text 1), which is based on Edward Hopper's picture.

- Does Julie O'Callaghan see the painting in the same way as you did?
- If you were to make up a *monologue* of this kind, showing what was going through the woman's mind, what do you think she might be be saying?

PICTURE 1

Context

Edward Hopper

Edward Hopper (1882–1967) was born in New York and lived there for most of his life. He is one of America's best-known painters. Almost all his paintings are pictures of buildings, and the people who inhabit them. Many of them look a bit like stills from a film. They are the sort of pictures that make people want to invent stories about them.

'Automat' was painted in 1927, and **'Sunlight in a Cafeteria'** (Picture 2) in 1958.

Context

Julie O'Callaghan

Julie O'Callaghan was born in Chicago, USA, but moved to Ireland in the 1970s where she has lived since. She has published several books of poetry. Her first book, *Edible Anecdotes*, contained a group of poems based on Hopper paintings.

TEXT 1

AUTOMAT

I thought when I came here
I'd get as rich as a secretary
and marry my boss.
I dreamt about that so long
I thought it would happen.
Maybe I should go back.

I hate small places though
and when I sit eating at the automat
I pretend I'm a celebrity
and all those walls of plastic doors
are really crowds of camera lenses
waiting to take my picture.

Julie O'Callaghan

B READING IMAGES

1 Now, working in pairs, take a look at the painting **'Sunlight in a Cafeteria'** (Picture 2). Would you have guessed that this picture is by the same artist? What is it about the painting that might give that impression?

- As before, try 'reading' this painting. What kind of place is this? What time of day? How would you describe the atmosphere?
- This time, there are two characters. Are they aware of each other?
- If this was a shot from a film, what do you think might have happened before this moment – and what might happen next?

2 Now read aloud Sujata Bhatt's poem (Text 2) based on this picture. One of you read part 1, and the other read part 2.

- Does the poem match the picture, do you think?

PICTURE 2

SUNLIGHT IN A CAFETERIA

1
The man thinks:
'What a lousy deal.
It'll take all day to fix that car.
I wish the heat would let up.
The kids will want to go
to the beach again.
I don't have the time for it.
Who'll paint the house?'

2
Meanwhile, at the other table,
          the woman thinks:
'It's July again.
What a month to spend in New York City.
What a month to be pregnant.
Why do they call it morning sickness
when it hits me in the afternoon as well?

And sometimes even at night
when I least suspect it.
This dress is already a bit tight
for me. I wish Jim would hurry up.
Can't stand the smell of that guy's cigarette.
Should I have another coffee?
I hope Jim likes my hair.
I didn't know New York would be
like this. I'm not ready for it.
July used to be my favourite month.
Always sunny. I'm glad I'm not in Denmark anymore.
I probably shouldn't sit in the sun
but I missed it so much over there.
I like this New York
July sunlight, it's so honest –
right to the point,
no misunderstandings.
I know where I stand.'

Sujata Bhatt

Context

Sujata Bhatt was born in India, but spent her student years in the USA, before moving to Germany, where she now lives. She writes mainly in English, but also in her mother-tongue, which is Gujarati. One of her books of poetry, *Monkey Shadows*, contains several poems based on paintings.

C CREATIVE WRITING

1 This is an individual writing task. Browse through some art books, in your school or local library, or visit a website with paintings, such as the Tate Gallery site (www.tate.org.uk). Find a painting which interests you. Then write a *monologue* poem based on the picture.

- It could be a single monologue, as in Julie O'Callaghan's poem. Or, if there are two people in the picture, you could create two monologues, in the way Sujata Bhatt has done.
- In either case, focus on the things that you think might be passing through the person's mind. What can they see? What mood are they in? What has recently happened, or what are they remembering from the past? What style of expression will you choose?
- If there are two people in your poem, think also about the different viewpoints they might take. Do they see things the same way? Or not?

Review

This unit has looked at paintings, at how people *'read'* visual images, and at the ways in which paintings can be converted into poems. We have focused on the interpretation of *character* and *setting* through *monologue* poems, and how both painters and poets create moods.

- As a class, talk about the difference between reading a painting and reading a poem.
- Listen to a reading aloud of one of the poems created during Activity C.

YEAR 8 UNIT 6

Do as I say

Aims

This unit looks at two texts (a scene from a playscript and a short story) based on parent-child dialogue. It considers the different ways in which these texts are written, and the tones established.

Starter session

As a class, brainstorm examples of parental instructions, such as tidying up, doing homework, worrying about health/social life/fashion tastes. Convert these into direct speech, using an imperative, and write them on the board. For example: *'Make sure you're home by nine o'clock…'*. Now discuss what might be said in response. Perform the dialogue you've created. One person delivers the instructions; another responds.

A READING AND DRAMA

1 In pairs, read aloud the scene from **'Skungpoomery'** (Text 1). Then talk briefly about the following:
   - What sort of people are these? Give each person an adjective.
   - This is the first page of the script – what style of play do you think it will be?
   - How might you change your reading aloud to emphasise the nature of the characters?
   - Now read the script aloud again.

Context

Ken Campbell

This is the opening page of a play for young audiences written in 1976 by Ken Campbell, a British playwright and performer who specialises in bizarre kinds of comedy. (The play's title, *Skungpoomery*, comes from a new system of vocabulary invented by characters in the play.)

SKUNGPOOMERY (extract)

P.C. NICHOLAS WIBBLE: But all the other policemen wear boots.
MRS. WIBBLE: That's because they haven't got nice sandals.
WIBBLE: Well why've I always got to be different?
MRS. WIBBLE: It's not a case of 'being different', Nicholas, it's a case of being sensible. It's unhealthy to have your feet laced up inside those big clumping boots all day in the hot weather –
WIBBLE: O Mum.
MRS. WIBBLE: I don't want to hear any more about it, Nicholas.
WIBBLE: Anyway those sandals pinch my feet, Mum.
MRS. WIBBLE: Nicholas! You little fibber! We got those sandals at Clarks and we both looked down the X-Ray machine together and we both saw that you had plenty of room in those sandals. Nicholas!
WIBBLE: Wh-at?
MRS. WIBBLE: What's that?
WIBBLE: What's what?
MRS. WIBBLE: On your tie?
WIBBLE: Nothing.
MRS. WIBBLE: Egg dribblings. Look at that. And I all nicely ironed it yesterday morning and now you've dribbled your egg on it. Come here. (*She leads him by his tie to the bowl and cloth.*)
WIBBLE: O Mum.
MRS. WIBBLE: O and it's not coming out look. It'll have to be put in soak.
WIBBLE: Oh no, Mum - look I'm due on the beat in five minutes. I can't wait while you soak it.
MRS. WIBBLE: Well I'm certainly not letting you go out with your tie in that state.
WIBBLE: The Sergeant gets really cross if I'm late.
MRS. WIBBLE: Well you'll just have to wear your bow-tie.
WIBBLE: O no.
MRS. WIBBLE: Nicholas!
WIBBLE: O look all the other policemen wear ordinary straight ties.
MRS. WIBBLE: Come here and let's put it on you and have less of your nonsense. Your Aunty Glad gave you this nice bow tie - and did you write her a proper thank you letter?
WIBBLE: Yes.
MRS. WIBBLE: Good boy. (*Looking at his face.*) Hanky? (*He supplies it.*) Lick. *He licks it and she wipes a bit of dirt off his face with it.*
WIBBLE: 'Bye then, Mum.

Ken Campbell

2 Ken Campbell, who wrote **'Skungpoomery'**, specialises in a particular kind of humour – absurd, bizarre, whacky. This scene seems to *parody* (or 'send up') both mother and child.
- What is there about this scene that reminds you of real life?
- What moves it away from reality?

3 Working in pairs, your next task is to improvise a short role-play between a parent and a child.
- It might be similar to the scene you've read, or quite different.
- But there must be something odd about at least one of the characters.
- So the role-play will be in some ways like real-life, but in some way *bizarre…*

B CRITICAL READING AND WRITING

Read Jamaica Kincaid's short story, **'Girl'** (Text 2). It's an unusual piece of writing, in a number of ways. Discuss it together as a class, or in small groups.

1 To begin with, focus for a moment on how it is structured.
- How many paragraphs are there?
- How many sentences?
- How many semicolons?
- Any other punctuation marks?
- Why are some bits in italics?
- Now have a careful look at the grammatical patterns. The semicolons divide the speech into around four dozen sections, each of which is a piece of *instruction* or *advice*. Look at how these instructions begin. Can you see any patterns here?

Context

Jamaica Kincaid

Jamaica Kincaid was born in Antigua, in the West Indies, later moving to New York to work as a journalist. She has written novels, short stories and a family biography, and is one of the Caribbean's most admired contemporary writers.

Vocabulary

benna: Caribbean folk-songs, considered unsuitable for singing on Sundays
wharf-rat boys: dock workers, sailors
okra: small green vegetable; also known as 'lady's fingers'
dasheen: leaf-vegetable
doukona: type of fruit pudding

GIRL

Wash the white clothes on Monday and put them on the stone heap; wash the color clothes on Tuesday and put them on the clothesline to dry; don't walk barehead in the hot sun; cook pumpkin fritters in very hot sweet oil; soak your little cloths right after you take them off; when buying cotton to make yourself a nice blouse, be sure that it doesn't have gum on it, because that way it won't hold up well after a wash; soak salt fish overnight before you cook it; is it true that you sing benna in Sunday school?; always eat your food in such a way that it won't turn someone else's stomach; on Sundays try to walk like a lady and not like the slut you are so bent on becoming; don't sing benna in Sunday school; you mustn't speak to wharf-rat boys, not even to give directions; don't eat fruits on the street – flies will follow you; *but I don't sing benna on Sundays at all and never in Sunday school*; this is how to sew on a button; this is how to make a buttonhole for the button you have just sewed on; this is how to hem a dress when you see the hem coming down and so to prevent yourself from looking like the slut I know you are so bent on becoming; this is how you iron your father's khaki shirt so that it doesn't have a crease; this is how you iron your father's khaki pants so that they don't have a crease; this is how you grow okra – far from the house, because okra tree harbors red ants; when you are growing dasheen, make sure it gets plenty of water or else it makes your throat itch when you are eating it; this is how you sweep a corner; this is how you sweep a whole house; this is how you sweep a yard; this is how you smile to someone you don't like too much; this is how you smile to someone you don't like at all; this is how you smile to someone you like completely; this is how you set a table for tea; this is how you set a table for dinner; this is how you set a table for dinner with an important guest; this is how you set a table for lunch; this is how you set a table for breakfast; this is how to behave in the presence of men who don't know you very well, and this way they won't recognize immediately the slut I have warned you against becoming; be sure to wash every day, even if it is with your own spit; don't squat down to play marbles – you are not a boy, you know; don't pick people's flowers – you might catch something; don't throw stones at blackbirds, because it might not be a blackbird at all; this is how to make a bread pudding; this is how to make doukona; this is how to make pepper pot; this is how to make a good medicine for a cold; this is how to make a good medicine to throw away a child before it even becomes a child; this is how to catch a fish; this is how to throw back a fish you don't like, and that way something bad won't fall on you; this is how to bully a man; this is how a man bullies you; this is how to love a man, and if this doesn't work there are other ways, and if they don't work don't feel too bad about giving up; this is how to spit up in the air if you feel like it, and this is how to move quick so that it doesn't fall on you; this is how to make ends meet; always squeeze bread to make sure it's fresh; *but what if the baker won't let me feel the bread?*; you mean to say that after all you are really going to be the kind of woman who the baker won't let near the bread?

Jamaica Kincaid

2. Jamaica Kincaid grew up on the island of Antigua, in the West Indies, during the 1950s.
   - What does the reader learn from this story about the way of life that she remembers?
   - What makes it different from your own way of life?
   - Is there anything that the mother says which does link with your own experience of childhood?

3. Your main task, working individually, is to write a short essay about the story you have been reading. Here is a suggested paragraph plan, based on the things so far discussed:
   - Introduction: text and context
   - Summary of what the story is about
   - Structure and style of writing
   - What the story tells you about the world in which it was written
   - What the story tells you about mothers and daughters

4. And here is an optional extra. Produce a short piece of writing, modelled on the one you have studied, in which a parent from your own culture instructs his or her child:
   - One sentence only
   - Lots of semicolons
   - Insert some italicised (or underlined) responses if you want…

Review

This unit has looked at two forms of parent-child *dialogue* – one a playscript, the other an unusual form of prose story. Both mothers are giving their children *instructions* on how they should behave, and the cultural *values* they believe are important. Both authors write in a *humourous* style, with an element of *parody*.

- What values do your own parents emphasise when they give you instructions or advice? If you had children of your age, what values would you emphasise to them?
- Listen to a reading aloud of one of the optional short stories created during Activity B.

YEAR 8 UNIT 7

First to speak

Aims

In this unit we will look at three versions of a traditional story, drawn from different times and places, and explore the different ways in which they are written.

Starter session

Your teacher will ask you, in turn, to do a series of imaginary tasks. When it is your turn, answer with either an excuse (*'I can't, because I've hurt my finger…'*), or a counter-argument (*'X should do it because they're nearer the door…'*). Be as ingenious as you can.

A   READING TO COMPARE

This activity could be done together as a class, or in groups.

1 Read the Indian folk story, **'The Quarrel'** (Text 1). What does it suggest about how couples sometimes behave?

2 Now read **'Get Up and Bar the Door'** (Text 2), which is in the form of a ballad, meaning that it would have originally been sung.

- This one will be harder to read because it's written in old Scottish *dialect* – but you should be able to work out the meaning of most of the lines if you try saying them aloud. Check the Vocabulary list where you need to.
- You also need to decide who speaks the final four lines, since the ballad doesn't actually tell us this.

3 When you've got the story clear in your mind, compare **'Get Up and Bar the Door'** with **'The Quarrel'**. Discuss the following:

- What are the *narrative* elements that connect the two stories?
- What are the differences between the two stories?
- What do the two married couples have in common?
- Think also about the difference in *form* between the two tales. Does the difference in form affect how the story comes over?

TEXT 1

THE QUARREL

In a tribal village there lived an old couple. Once they had a quarrel over food. The old woman had prepared seven *bhakris*, and the quarrel arose over how they would be divided. The wife said:

'I have prepared them, so I shall have more.'

But the husband said:

'I have paid for them, so I must have more.'

They quarrelled till they were both exhausted. Then they lay down to sleep leaving the supper uneaten. At midnight, the old man sat up and said:

'Let us come to terms. Whoever speaks first will have three, and whoever keeps silent longer will have four.'

They agreed to this and lay down again and kept silent. Not a word all night. Dawn broke, yet no word passed between them. The day and night passed. Yet both kept mum. Thus two days passed away. No sound came from their house.

Neighbours thought it strange.

'What's happened to the old couple?' they said.

They went and knocked at the door. There was no response. Then they forced open the door and found both lying on the floor, eyes closed. Two days of hunger had made them pale and weak. The neighbours went near and asked:

'Eh, old man, is anything wrong?'

No reply came, so they went to the wife. But she too did not move. So the neighbours thought that they were dead. They made arrangements for their funeral and when they were complete they placed them on the bier and took them to the graveyard. Even then the couples did not utter a word. But when their bodies were being lowered into the grave, the wife quietly said:

'Alright, I will eat three, you can have four.'

Traditional: Maharashtra (India)

Vocabulary

bhakris: fried bread-cakes, parathas

keep mum: stay silent

bier: frame for carrying a body to a grave; traditional across many countries.

Context

This traditional oral tale comes from Maharashtra, the west-coast region of India which includes Bombay and Goa. It was written down in the twentieth century, but has been told orally for much longer. This version was translated into English by Indumati Sheorey.

TEXT 2

GET UP AND BAR THE DOOR

There livd a man in yonder glen
And John Blunt was his name;
He maks gude malt and he brews gude ale,
And he bears a wondrous fame.

It happened about Martinmas,
And a gay time it was then,
When John Blunt's wife had puddings to make,
And she's boild them in the pan.

The wind it blew frae north to south,
It blew into the floor;
Says auld John Blunt to his gude wife,
'Get up, and bar the door.'

'My hans are in my hussyfskep,
I canna weel get them free,
And if ye dinna bar it yersel
It'll never be barred by me.'

They made a pact atween them twa,
They made it firm and sure.
Whoeer should speak the foremost word
Should rise and bar the door.

There was twa travellers travelling late,
Came riding cross the moor,
And they entered into John Blunt's house
By the light of the open door.

First they said gude een to them,
And then they spak some more,
But neer a word would the auld folk say
For the barring o' the door.

And first they ate the white puddings,
And then they ate the black,
And next they drank the auld man's ale,
Yet neer a word he spak.

Then said the one unto the other,
'Here, man, tak ye my knife,
Do ye scrape aff the auld man's beard,
And I'll kiss the gudewife.'

'Ye hae eaten my food, ye hae drunken my drink,
And ye'll mak my gudewife a whore!'
'John Blunt, ye hae spoken the foremost word,
Get up and bar the door.'

Traditional: Scotland

Context

'Get Up and Bar the Door' is a traditional Scottish oral ballad. Ballads of this kind were memorised and passed on to other singers. No one can be sure when this one began to be sung. The earliest written versions, on which this one is based, were published in the eighteenth century. Versions are still sung by Scottish and English folk singers.

Vocabulary

yonder: 'over there'

glen: mountain valley

malt: malt whisky

Martinmas: Nov 11th – traditional Scottish feast-day

gay: happy, enjoyable (old meaning)

gudewife: 'goodwife' was a traditional way of saying 'wife'

hussyfskep: houseware, utensils

whore: old English word for an immoral woman

B WRITING OR SPEAKING

The version of **'The Quarrel'** given at the start of this unit is actually only half the story. In the full version, the old couple are carried to the grave by seven neighbours. After the wife has finally spoken, the story continues: 'As soon as the seven neighbours heard these words…

1 Take another look at this tale, and decide how you think it could continue. Then write or tell the new version.
   - If you decide to write it, add another page or so, starting with the quotation given above.
   - If you decide to tell the tale, then try re-telling it from the beginning. If you want, you could work in pairs: divide the story into chunks, and decide who will tell which. Rehearse it a couple of times, then tell it to a small audience. You don't need to memorise the sentences exactly, as long as the plot of the story comes out as you have planned it.

C READING AND SPEAKING

Oral versions of the story we have been studying have been recorded in most European countries, and in China, Turkey, Brazil, and Spanish America, as well as India.

Here's one more variation, called **'The Jamming Pan'** (Text 3). This one was recorded in 1932, as told by a storyteller from the village of Crosthwaite, in Cumbria.

As you'll discover, the person who recorded this version has *transcribed* what was said – that is, written the words down in a way that shows how the speaker said them.

1 Working in a group of four or five, prepare a reading aloud of **'The Jamming Pan'**.
   - Divide the roles between you.
   - You'll have to work out what you think each character is saying, and what mood they are in – as well as how you think their accents should sound.

TEXT 3

THE JAMMING PAN

There was a farm-house a long way from anywheres, about five or six miles from t'nearest house. At this farm they'd a terrible lot of fruit trees, and damson time had come round again, and they were short of a brass pan for jamming with.

So t'ald farmer says ya day: 'Eh, lass, I want thee te ga down to ald Jack Sowerby's an' git their brass pan.'

T'lass says: 'Nay, hang it. I's nut gaan fer a thing like that five mile. Neea, nut I.'

So he went til his wife an' said: 'Hey, Libby! thee slip down to ald mother Sowerby's an' esk her for t'brass pan. Tell here we're gaan te jam.'

'Nae damn fear!' she says. 'I's nut gaan if jammin' nivver gits done!'

An' he says: 'Ye stupid ald beggar, ye. What thee an' t' lass? It looks damn like I shall hev te ga mysel.' So he started off for it after they'd milked ya neet.

Efter aw t'jammin' had gitten done it was time for t'pan te ga back again. But t'question was, wha was gaan te tek it? So t'ald farmer says: 'Ah'll tell ye what ah'll do: which yan o' us speeaks after now this verra minute hes t'pan te tek back,' he says, 'an' I's damn sure it'll nut be me!' Then the silence began.

The family went to bed, nobody saying owt. Next mornin' they aw gat up – still t'tongues was quiet. Aw went like that till drinkin' time. Then there was a girt rattle on t'dooer. Neeabody answered it. So this here chap walked in – he was a girt big roadster – a bad lookin' sort of a chap he was – he says: 'Good mornin' – grand mornin'.' Still silence, so he collared a girt lump o' pasty an' hed a pint o' tea. Aw was still silent, so he crammed his belly as full as he could git it. He had a peep in yan o' t'drawers, spot' a ten bob note and pocket' it. Still silence amongst the others. So he walks up to t'ald woman.

'By gum!' he says, 'Ye're a smart lookin' woman. D'ye mind if I gi'e ye a kiss?' Still silence, so he gev her yan.

Then he walks up to t'lass, he says: 'By gum! thou's as good a lookin' as thi mother. Dosta mind if I gi'e thee yan?' He was a bit capped that nothing was said after all he'd done. So he gave her a kiss.

Then he turned t'ald farmer: 'Na, come on. It's thy turn now!'

T'ald farmer said: 'Nay, damn it. I'll tek t'pan back!'

Traditional: Northern England

Review

This unit has compared three versions of a similar story, drawn from different times and places. One was *translated* from an Indian language, one written in an eighteenth-century Scottish *dialect*, and the third transcribed from a spoken English *regional dialect*. Also, one of the versions took the form of a *ballad*, while the other two were *prose* stories.

- As a class, talk over how much the stories had in common, and what made them different. Were these differences mainly a question of dialect, or of form and style, or of subject matter?
- Listen to a reading or telling of one of the stories created during Activity B.

YEAR 8 UNIT 8

Animal magic

Aims

This unit explores three poems (and a painting) which represent natural creatures, but in a figurative way. The activities focus on how these works have been created, and the impressions they give.

Starter session

Your teacher will allocate each of you a letter of the alphabet (though not 'x'…). You need to create a simile using the following pattern:

As active as an ant…
As bold as a baboon…
As crafty as a crocodile…

Choose any creatures you like – birds, fish, insects. Try and come up with an adjective you don't normally use. Include two if you like: *As doleful and dumb-founded as a diplodocus*… . Read your phrase to the class.

A CRITICAL READING

1. As a class, read **'Mythic Animals'** (Text 1) by Norman Silver.

2. Then with closed eyes, listen to a second (slowed down) reading from your teacher, and try to form an *image* in your mind of each of the creatures described.

3. Let's now look at the *structure* of this poem. What could we say about each of the following:
   - Its verse-form
   - Its punctuation
   - Its sentence grammar
   - Its use of connectives.

   Jot down a brief note about each.

4. The poem begins with what seems to be a clear *statement*. What happens to this statement as the poem continues?

5 Decide how you would summarise, in one short sentence, what this poem is saying about animals?

Some of the things the poem says about these six animals are factually accurate. Others are not *literally* true – e.g. zebras do not wear Newcastle football shirts – but are true in some other way: the poem is using *figurative* (or 'metaphorical') language.

6 In pairs, decide on three things we learn from the poem about these creatures which are literally true ('A (crab) has…'), and three things which are figuratively true.

TEXT 1

MYTHIC ANIMALS

No creature
is more astonishing
than the unicorn
with its magical spiral horn

unless it's a crab
with six pairs of jaws
sideways scuttle
and eyes at the ends of stalks

or perhaps a bat
with membrane between
its elongated fingers
hanging upside-down like an umbrella

or a zebra
with its fingerprint face
and Newcastle United
football shirt

or a hummingbird
that can fly backwards
with wings vibrating
a hundred beats per second

or a dolphin
with Buddha smile
performing a series of aerial leaps
as if to say farewell.

Norman Silver

Vocabulary

mythic: unreal; existing only in myths (ancient supernatural tales)

unicorn: an imaginary creature – a small horse with a single projecting horn – which appears in myths from various cultures

Buddha: the founder of the Indian faith of Buddhism – usually pictured with a smiling face

Context

Norman Silver

Norman Silver was born in Cape Town, South Africa. He moved to England in 1969. He has written a number of engaging books of poetry for young people, including *The Walkmen Have Landed* (Faber) from which 'Mythic Animals' is taken.

B CRITICAL READING

The other poems in this unit also describe creatures in imaginative and figurative ways.

1 Read **'The Locust'** (Text 2), a poem originating from Madagascar, in Africa.
   - Now draw a locust, based on what you have read. (You have 5 minutes to do this.)

2 Scanning through the punctuation marks helps us to get a sense of the poem's structure. It starts with a question, and the answer is a series of statements, separated by semicolons or full stops. These two punctuation marks have a similar function, but full stops are more definite – so it's worth thinking about why the writer has chosen full stops in certain places.

   We could also say that the answer to the opening question – 'What is a locust?' – comes in the form of a string of metaphors. (Note that two of these are technically 'similes'.)
   - When you put all these metaphors together, what impression of locusts do you get?

3 Now read Gillian Clarke's **'Chip-hog'** (Text 3).
   - How easy did you find it to work out which animal the poet is describing? What were the clearest clues?
   - What figurative descriptions do you notice?
   - If we checked which punctuation marks appear most often in this poem, one answer would be hyphens. Hyphens are often used to join words together to create a new word.

   Look at these new creations:

   'leaf-scuffer'
   'Milk-scrounger'
   'slug-scavenger'.

   What do they have in common, in terms of their construction? (Notice that 'to scuff', 'to scrounge' and 'to scavenge' are all verbs.)
   - Or what about these?

   'Hog-of-the-road'
   'eye-in-the-leaf-pile'

   Hyphenated words or phrases of this sort were a strong tradition in medieval English poetry. There's an old form of poem called a *kenning* which consists of a set of descriptive phrases of this kind, which Gillian Clarke is echoing here.

4 Another traditional technique which this poet uses is *alliteration* – choosing words which start with the same consonant.
- Read through the poem again aloud, and listen out for the points where the alliteration affects the way the poem sounds.
- Are there any other ways in which this poem uses some form of repetition?

TEXT 2

THE LOCUST

What is a locust?
Its head, a grain of corn; its neck, the hinge of a knife;
Its horns, a bit of thread; its chest is smooth and burnished;
Its body is like a knife-handle;
Its hock, a saw; its spittle, ink;
Its underwings, clothing for the dead.
On the ground – it is laying eggs;
In flight – it is like the clouds.
Approaching the ground, it is rain glittering in the sun;
Lighting on a plant, it becomes a pair of scissors;
Walking, it becomes a razor;
Desolation walks with it.

Traditional: Malagasy (Madagascar)

Vocabulary

burnished: polished
hock: knee-bone
desolation: destruction, despair.

Context

This translated poem comes from Madagascar, off the eastern coast of Africa. It is not known who composed it: it was published in a book called *The Unwritten Song*, a collection of anonymous, orally remembered songs and poems. The locust is an insect, native to sub-tropical areas, which can cause extensive damage to crops.

Context

Gillian Clarke is a Welsh poet who writes in English. Her poetry for adult readers is widely admired, and popular in secondary schools. 'Chip-hog' is from a book of poems for younger readers called *The Animal Wall*.

Vocabulary

to hunker: to squat down
rosary: string of beads (used by Catholics for counting prayers)

TEXT 3

CHIP-HOG

Hog-of-the-road,
leaf-scuffer,
little tramp of the lanes —

like the old bearded one
wheel-wobbling his bicycle,
weighed to the saddle
with string bags, ropes
a rosary of tin mugs,
or hunkered down for the winter
under threadbare thatch.

Pin-cushion,
boot-brush,
flea-bag,
eye-in-the-leaf-pile.

One fifth of November
we lifted him just in time,
safe on a shovel from the smoke
of his smouldering house,
his spines sparking like stars.

Milk-scrounger,
slug-scavenger,
haunter of back doors and bins.

Once, kissing goodnight at the gate,
we saw a ghost:
something white,
something small,
something scratching,
headlong, hell-bent, heel-over-tip hedgehog,
head in a chip-bag and hooked
on his own prickles,
the last chip escaping him
as fast as he could run.

Gillian Clarke

PICTURE 1

Context

José Garcia Cordero

The painter José Garcia Cordero is from the Spanish-speaking Dominican Republic, in the West Indies. He has produced a series of paintings in which 'dogs' have been converted into strange figurative images.

Vocabulary

'Bilingual' (adj.) means 'able to speak two languages.'

'Tongue' is a word that has two meanings, though they are closely related. In the first place, it means that bit of our mouth which we use to taste things, or to help us speak. But just as common is the more abstract meaning that has developed out of that: your 'tongue' is also the language you speak in, and the things you say.

When joined by a hyphen to another word, the word 'double' often carries a rather sinister meaning – think of 'double-cross', 'double-dealing', or 'double-talk.' 'Double-tongued' has a similar feel to it. The dictionary says it means 'deceitful of speech'.

In the same way, to 'speak with forked tongue' means to deceive by saying one thing to one person, but a different thing to someone else. A 'forked tongue' is what snakes have.

C CREATIVE WRITING

1 Look at the painting by José Garcia Cordero called **'Bilingual Dog'** (Picture 1). Talk about what you see, and the impression it makes.

2 Read the selection of Vocabulary notes below the picture. Do any of these notes give you an idea about Cordero's painting?

3 Write a poem about a 'Bilingual Dog'.
- Change the title if you want to.
- The poem can be about other things as well as this painting – you could introduce more strange animals, for example.
- Think also about the style of your poem, and the kind of figurative language you might use.
- See if any of the poems in this unit give you an idea about how you could write your own poem (verse-form? alliteration? hyphenated phrases?).

Review

This unit has been partly about animals and how we perceive them, but the activities have focused on *poetic form*. We have looked at *imagery*, and the difference between *literal* and *figurative* images; at verse structure, repetition and other patterning; at how poets use *punctuation*; at the creation of *hyphenated* words and phrases; and at the use of *alliteration*.

- As a class, talk about the things poets do with language that you have learned about during this unit. Have you included any of these things in your own writing?
- Listen to a reading aloud of one of the poems created during Activity C.

YEAR 8 UNIT 9

Colours

Aims

This unit looks at an assortment of poems about colours, and focuses on the connotations which colours develop. It also considers some of the ways in which poems imply values, including the use of irony.

Starter session

Take a look at the colour chart. Actually, it's a non-colour chart, because it has been reproduced here in black and white. But in the original, each of the four columns contains a single colour – pale at the top, dark at the bottom. Which colours are they?

The clues, of course, are in the various names the colours have been given, and the *associations* these names carry.

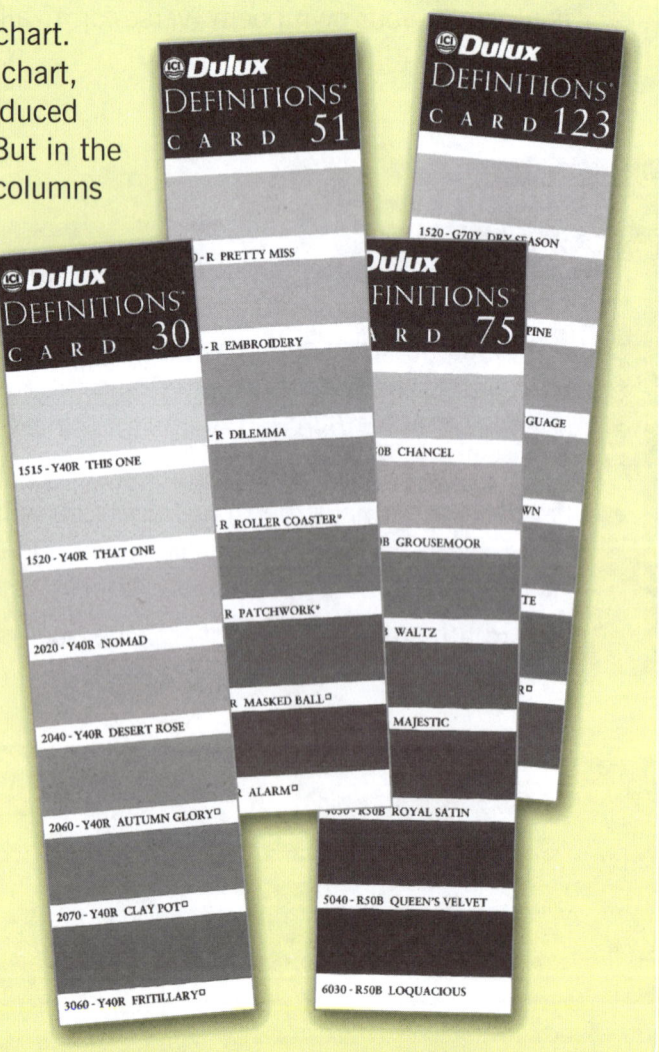

Dulux DEFINITIONS CARD 51
- R PRETTY MISS
- R EMBROIDERY
- R DILEMMA
- R ROLLER COASTER*
- R PATCHWORK*
- R MASKED BALL□
- R ALARM□

Dulux DEFINITIONS CARD 123
1520 - G70Y DRY SEASON

Dulux DEFINITIONS CARD 30
1515 - Y40R THIS ONE
1520 - Y40R THAT ONE
2020 - Y40R NOMAD
2040 - Y40R DESERT ROSE
2060 - Y40R AUTUMN GLORY□
2070 - Y40R CLAY POT
3060 - Y40R FRITILLARY□

Dulux DEFINITIONS CARD 75
- PINE
- 0B CHANCEL
- 0B GROUSEMOOR
- WALTZ
- MAJESTIC
- R50B ROYAL SATIN
- 5040 - R50B QUEEN'S VELVET
- 6030 - R50B LOQUACIOUS

- GUAGE
- WN
- TE
- R□

50

A CRITICAL READING

1 Colours often carry strong associations for us, both public and personal. What does **'Yellow'** make you think of, for example?
Or **'Red'**? Read the poems with these titles written by Helen Dunmore (Text 1) and Grace Nichols (Text 2).
- What do these colours *mean* to these poets? What feelings do they evoke?

TEXT 1

YELLOW

Think of something yellow.

The sun?
A fat ripe pear
or buttercup petals?

Yellow is butter.
Yellow is custard.
Yellow is egg-yolks.

Yellow has all the answers.
Yellow is like
an advert that twists your eyes
till they light on yellow.

What is yellow?

Nobody answered.
Shakeela smiled
and stroked her yellow
shalwar khameez
so butterly
and buttercuply
that all our fingers turned yellow.

Helen Dunmore

Vocabulary

shalwar khameez: trousers and top (South Asian)

Context

Helen Dunmore is an English poet and novelist whose work is widely read and admired. This poem comes from a book of poems for young people called *Secrets*.

TEXT 2

RED

Red as the colour
I sometime paint my nails,
ten archway windows
in sacramental stain.

Red as hibiscus
and flametree I love,
the brackish red sorrel
that stained me like blood.

That this same red
should be so readily shed,
so easily splattered by butchers
and bombers and childface soldiers.

This red without which
we whiteout forever.

Grace Nichols

Vocabulary

sacramental: holy, religiously ceremonial
hibiscus: crimson flowering shrub, found in sub-tropical countries
flametree: another sub-tropical plant with vivid red flowers
brackish: salt-watery, leaving a stain
red sorrel: herbal plant used for cookery and medicine
whiteout: faint, pass out

Context

Grace Nichols

Grace Nichols was born in Guyana, in the West Indies, and has lived in England since the 1970s. Her books of poems, both for adult and younger readers, are enjoyable and thought-provoking, and have contributed valuably to the development of cultural diversity in schools.

2 Look again at the first half of **'Yellow'**, then write a brief poem of your own using some of Helen Dunmore's lines as a model (e.g. 'Orange is…' or 'Purple is like…').

- Include three different colours, and create three lines for each colour.
- Your choice of images should make it clear what each colour means to you.
- It may be that for you, as for Grace Nichols, some colours have both positive and negative associations.

B READING AND CREATIVE WRITING

All words carry *literal* meanings. In addition, many words carry further suggestions – *connotations* – which can be either *positive* or *negative*. This is one reason why we sometimes have to think carefully about the words we choose.

Two colours with a particularly strong range of connotations are 'black' and 'white'.

1 Let's look first at how these colours appear in a thesaurus (Text 3).
- What differences do you notice between the connotations these two words seem to carry?
- Can you think how this has come about?

TEXT 3

ROGET'S THESAURUS (extract)

white (adj.)

white, pure; dazzling, light, bright, luminous; silvery, alabaster, marble; chalky, snowy, frosty; soapy, lathery; white as a lily, white as milk, white as a sheet, white as the driven snow; pure white, lily-white, milk-white, snow-white, whitewashed, clean; whitish, pearly, creamy, ivory, waxen, pale, off-white, colourless; blonde, fair, Nordic, ash-blonde, platinum-blonde, fair-haired.

black (adj.)

black, sable, inky, pitch-black, black as thunder; sooty, smokey, smutty, dirty; blackened, charred; black-haired, raven-haired, brunette; black-skinned, Negroid; coloured; sombre, gloomy; coal-black, black as ink, black as pitch, black as the ace of spades, black as hell; black as night; blackish, swarthy, black-faced, dusky, dark, dark-skinned; black and blue; low-toned.

2 Now read through the extract from **'Dictionary Black'** (Text 4), by the British poet Sista Roots, which explores these connotations directly. The poem is based on a set of words or phrases beginning with 'black'.

Sista Roots writes poems to be performed aloud, so their *tone* is important. In pairs, experiment with ways of reading **'Dictionary Black'** aloud:
- How will you divide the poem into two voices?
- What tone of voice will you use?
- Will the tone vary from verse to verse?

3 Next, open a dictionary – the larger the better – and go to the page containing the word 'black'.
- Does it contain any of the words which Sista Roots found in her dictionary?
- Are there any other words or phrases with negative connotations which the poet could have referred to?
- Which words or phrases carry positive connotations?

4 Now turn to the page containing the word 'white', and explore the words and phrases – and their connotations – which you find there.

5 Finally, write an extra verse or two about the connotations of 'white' to complete this poem.
- Use some of the words you have researched.
- You could start with Sista Roots' lines: 'I knew what next to sight / So I turn to 'White'…' Or you could start with your own words.
- Think about the tone in which the lines will be spoken.
- How will you end the poem? What do you want to leave the audience thinking?

Context

Sista Roots

Sista Roots is an Afro-British performance-poet. **'Dictionary Black'** was published in the 1980s in a collection of poems by black women writers called *Watchers & Seekers* (Women's Press).

DICTIONARY BLACK (extract)

I was looking through my dictionary
Just the other day
And in front of my eyes
Though I was not surprised
Was a list as long as my back
Giving literal form & fact
To all those words
Containing 'Black'

The first thing it says is
Opposite to white
I say to myself
Mmhmm alright
It says
Blackhearted – dismal – grim –
Angry – threatening
Black looks
Black marks
Black lists
And Black books.

Deadly – sinister – wicked – hateful
All these words to make us 'grateful'?

A kidnapped Negro on a slaveship
Is a Blackbird
(I thought they did have wing
Eat worm and sing and t'ing)
Blackbirding is the trade itself
That gave these people enormous wealth
Blackcap is what you get
When sentenced to death
Black Maria – Blackmail – Black Death –
Hold on a sec
Let me take a break
I haven't finished yet

So just for a lark
I check out 'dark'
Well guess what it says
It says Black
More or less

A Darky is a Negro
Not fair – atrocious – evil –
And the Prince of Darkness
Is the Devil
And of course
Africa is that continent dark
(Where all those blackbirds did embark)

You want to hear more?
Well, guess what else…
You can darken one's door
I knew what next to sight
So I turn to 'White'…

Sista Roots

C CRITICAL READING

This unit will end with a writing task, in which you are asked to write about any two of the colour poems you have read. Here are two more you might choose.

1 Bearing in mind what we have discussed so far, see what you make of Benjamin Zephaniah's poem **'White Comedy'** (Text 5). Here's a clue: the dictionary defines 'black comedy' as 'making a joke of tragic or unpleasant aspects of life'. With that as a starting point, can you work out what the poet is up to?

2 The final poem in this selection is John Agard's **'Anancy's Thoughts on Colours'** (Text 6). Anancy is the name of a spider who appears in a huge number of African and Caribbean myths and folk tales. Anancy is a *trickster* – a cunning character, who always finds a way to get the better of the other animals, however grand and powerful they might be. Why would Anancy decide to remain 'original dark', do you think?

TEXT 5

WHITE COMEDY

I waz whitemailed
By a white witch,
Wid white magic
An white lies,
Branded a white sheep
I slaved as a whitesmith
Near a white spot
Where I suffered whitewater fever.
Whitelisted as a white leg
I waz in de white book
As a master of de white art,
It waz like white death.

People call me white jack
Some hailed me as white wog,
So I joined de white watch
Trained as a white guard
Lived off de white economy.
Caught an beaten by de whiteshirts

I waz condemned to a white mass.
Don't worry,
I shall be writing to de Black House.

Benjamin Zephaniah

Context

Benjamin Zephaniah is one of Britain's most popular poets. He writes and performs poems both for adults and young people, and his work is available both in books and on CDs. Born in Birmingham, he grew up in Jamaica and in Handsworth, and many of his poems are written in a form of Caribbean English dialect. **'White Comedy'** is from one of Zephaniah's books for adult readers, called *Propa Propaganda*.

TEXT **6**

ANANCY'S THOUGHTS ON COLOURS

Long-time back in the beginning beginning
when sky-god Nyame was handing out colour,
sky-god Nyame take one look at me Anancy
and say pick whichever colour you fancy.

I cast me eye high
I cast me eye low
I work up me brain to studify
dis colour issue,
spare it a thought or two.

Red stare at me from deep gash of skin
Yellow try to tempt me with sunflower grin
Green wink at me with brazen leaf-eye
White beckon me with subtle shift of cloud.
And all dis time blue so damn calm and proud
as if one shimmer and Anancy done blue.

I work up me brain good-good.
I turn to sky-god Nyame.
I say sky-god Nyame, I done ponder
dis thing you call colour issue.
Thank you but no thank you.

Let Snake, Tiger, Parrot and dem
hustle up for colour hand-out.
I will stay original dark
as it was in the beginning beginning,
spinning web of bright imagining,
cherishing the gift of cunning.

John Agard

Vocabulary

studify: 'studify' is an invented word – but not hard to guess?
brazen: 'bold as brass', shameless
ponder: think about

Context

John Agard

John Agard, born in Guyana, in the West Indies, is a very popular poetry-performer who has produced a range of books both for adult and younger readers. This poem is taken from *Weblines* (Bloodaxe), a collection which explores the rich territory of Afro-Caribbean mythology, including the stories of the trickster spider-god, Anancy. Many of Agard's poems, as here, are written in Caribbean dialect.

D CRITICAL WRITING

Finally, here is your individual writing task:

1 Choose two poems from this unit (your teacher may wish to advise you which ones to choose) and write a short essay called 'Two colour poems', based on what you have read and discussed during this unit.

Here is a possible plan:
- Write six paragraphs, say two to three sentences per paragraph.
- Introduce the theme of colour. (So you might start 'One of the interesting things about colours is…'.)
- Explain the meaning of the first poem. For example, 'In Sista Roots' poem **'Black Dictionary'**, the poet writes about what she discovered when…'.
- Then comment on how the poem is written.
- Explain the meaning of the second poem.
- Then comment how the poem is written. For example, 'When you first read Zephaniah's poem, it seems odd because…'.
- Conclude your essay by explaining what these two poems left you thinking about colour, or language, or poetry – or all three. If you can, try and bring in the term 'connotation'.

Review

This unit has explored a variety of poems on the subject of colour, both in terms of the *personal associations* which we attach to them, and in terms of the more general *connotations* which colours have developed, particularly in the case of black and white.

- As a class, make a short list of colours and decide on the kind of associations they carry. Can you divide the list into those with broadly positive, and those with broadly negative connotations? Or is there disagreement on this?
- Listen to a reading aloud of one of the poems created during Activity A or B.

YEAR 8 UNIT 10

Money

Aims

This unit looks at scenes from a medieval European play, **'Everyman'**, and an African adaptation of the same play written in the twentieth century. We'll look at the style in which the plays are written, and how a story crosses from one continent (and century) to another. Then we'll try doing the same by creating our own local version of one of the stories.

Starter session

Your teacher will divide the board in two and will label one half 'Rich' and the other 'Poor'. Treat each space as a thesaurus entry, and think of as many words as you can to go into each. Include personal associations as well as vocabulary connections. Give your teacher your words to put on the board. When you have finished, talk about the words you have collected.

A READING FOR MEANING

1. Work in pairs. Look at the speech by God which comes at the beginning of the Middle English play **'Everyman'** (Text 1). Try to decide how to read it aloud. Does it make more sense when you hear it than when you see it?

2. Now take one of the speech's three sections, and jot down a translation into modern English. Despite the odd spellings, you'll probably find you know most of the words, and will be able to guess some of the others. The Vocabulary box gives you one or two clues.

3. When all pairs have finished, compare some of the new versions as a class, and decide together what God has to say about human beings in this speech.

TEXT 1

MIDDLE ENGLISH 'EVERYMAN' (extract)

GOD: I perceyve, here in my maieste,
     How that all creatures be to me unkynde,
     Lyvynge without drede in worldly prosperyte.
     Of ghostly syght the people be so blynde,
     Drowned in synne, they know me not for theyr God.
     In worldely ryches is all theyr mynde;
     They fere not my ryghtwysnes, the sharpe rod.

     They use the seven deedly synnes dampnable,
     As pryde, coveytyse, wrath, and lechery
     Now in the worlde be made commendable;
     And thus they leve of aungelles the hevenly company.
     Every man lyveth so after his owne pleasure,
     And yet of theyr lyfe they be nothynge sure.

     I se the more that I them forbere
     The worse they be fro yere to yere.
     They be so combred with worldly ryches
     That nedes on them I must do iustyce,
     On every man lyvynge without fere.
     Where arte thou, Deth, thou myghty messengere?

Anon

Vocabulary

(using modern spellings)

righteousness: justice, goodness

covetousness: greediness

lechery: sexual activity, randiness

forbear: tolerate, go easy on

(en)cumbered: loaded down

Context

'Everyman' was one of the very first English plays to be printed. It was written at the beginning of the sixteenth century by an unknown (anonymous) author. There is an old Dutch version of the same story, written at about the same time – no one is sure which version came first. European plays from the Middle Ages are almost all about religious subjects, and God often appears as a character.

The plot of **'Everyman'** goes like this. Displeased with Everyman's behaviour, God sends Death to call him to account – to decide whether he deserves to go to Heaven or to Hell. As Everyman's friends discover what is going on, they desert him. (The friends have names like Goods and Riches, Strength, Beauty.) The only two who are prepared to stay with him, and to make a case before God, are Knowledge and Good Deeds – and in the end, these are the friends who enable him to reach Heaven.

B READING AND DISCUSSION

1. As a class, read the first extract from the Nigerian version of **'Everyman'** (Text 2), which comes from near the beginning of the play. Then talk about the following:
   - What do you learn from this scene about the character of Everyman?
   - How much sympathy do you feel for him?
   - What do you make of Companion?
   - Can you make a connection between this scene and God's speech in Activity A?

2. Then read the second extract from the Nigerian **'Everyman'** (Text 3). At this late stage in the play, all Everyman's friends have deserted him, having learned that Iku (Death) is about to arrive to take Everyman to the God Olodumare (see Context notes). 'Owo' is Yoruban for 'money', so this figure is *personified*: he represents an *abstract* idea.

   In pairs, discuss the following:
   - How has Everyman changed since the earlier scene?
   - How has the playwright made 'Money' into a person?
   - Finally, write some notes in answer to this question:
     What have you learned, from these two extracts, about the world in which the characters live?

TEXT 2

NIGERIAN 'EVERYMAN' (extract 1)

In front of Everyman's house.
EVERYMAN has been talking with his COMPANION. The POOR NEIGHBOUR emerges from the background, and approaches fearfully.

EVERYMAN: You my friend and companion of many years,
(*to his companion*) Take this money, and hurry down to Bisi
My lady-lover. Tell her to come to my party
And bring the best Highlife band
She can find. And give her these few notes
For these independent women and
Lip-painted ladies have many needs

[continued over page]

And great pride. Let her go and buy
What she desires and let her heart
Be happy when she comes. This money
Will get her velvet cloth, rekyi rekyi,
Sarasobia scent, fine pomade, gold and silver,
Head-tie, handkerchiefs, umbrella, shoes,
Shirt and blouse, iron bed, blanket and
Bed sheets, pillows and pillow-cases,
Sleeping-gowns, easy chairs, door blinds,
Window blinds, mosquito-net, table and
Table-cloth, carpets, bed curtains,
Handwatch, looking-glass, powder,
Sewing-machine, portmanteaux, trunk box,
Bicycle, gramophone and so many other
Things a woman could use.

POOR NEIGHBOUR: Master, I beg you, help me
(*prostrates himself*) I am in trouble.

COMPANION: Do you know this man?

EVERYMAN: Who are you? I don't remember
Seeing you before.

POOR NEIGHBOUR: I am Adeleke, Sir, the son of Kunle.
I have known better days than these, Sir.
I was your neighbour, once,
Lived in that pretty house right next door.
But I ran into debt and was driven out!

EVERYMAN: All right, all right! (*He hands him a coin.*)

POOR NEIGHBOUR: Threepence?
(*refusing to take it*) That is a poor gift. If you would
Share that wad of notes with me,
My worries could be over.

EVERYMAN: Ah-ah? Is that all?

COMPANION: If you gave him that,
You would have a thousand beggars
After you tomorrow!

POOR NEIGHBOUR: This money, I know, is nothing to you.
If you spend it ten times over,
You only need to beckon your servant,
And he'll bring you the same amount from your house.

EVERYMAN: You foolish man!
Do you know what it means to be a rich man?
Do you think it is easy?
'A rich man!' That is easily said.
But we rich people lead a hard life,
If you knew it,
You might not want to change with me.
My money can never sit still:
It must run here and there,
Work for me and travel and fight.
Money must marry more money
And get pregnant with more money.
A rich man has no easy life:
His lorries break down
And want to be mended.
The price of cocoa falls
And petrol goes up.
One's children go to school
They study abroad, their dowry
Must be paid when they marry.
Do you think it is easy to maintain
All these houses and cars and farms
The children and wives and servants?
Do you think that money grows on a tree?
No work is harder than collecting debts and rents!
If I would listen to fellows like you,
I could not make three steps
Without opening my hand.
You think it is easy! But suppose
All my property was divided equally
Among all those who are in need –
Do you think your share would be bigger,
Than these three pence here?

Vocabulary

to prostrate yourself: to lie down before someone's feet
Highlife: West African dance music
rekyi rekyi: neckwear
sarasobia: type of perfume
pomade: scented ointment
portmanteaux: travelling cases
gramophone: machine for playing music
dowry: gift of money traditionally paid to a bridegroom by the bride's parent
Iku: Death (see context)
Owo: Money (see context)
harlot: old word for prostitute or paid mistress

[continued over page]

EVERYMAN throws down the threepence.
The POOR NEIGHBOUR picks it up and leaves.

COMPANION: You answered him well,
You put him in his place!
Money makes a man wise,
I can see that indeed.

Obotunde Ijimere

Context

This version of **'Everyman'** was written in the 1960s by Nigerian playwright Obotunde Ijimere, who writes in both Yoruban and English. Ijimere's version is actually based on an early-twentieth-century German adaptation of the play – this is a play that has been adapted into a number of different versions.

In this Nigerian version, Everyman is a wealthy, powerful character – what we might now call a 'fat cat' – who has devoted his whole life to money-making. In Text 2, near the beginning of the play, he has not yet learned that Olodumare, the Yoruban god of heaven, has sent Iku (Death) to bring Everyman to trial. In this version of the play, the ancient Christian belief that the dead are sent either to Heaven or to Hell is replaced by the Yoruban belief in reincarnation, or returning after death in a different form – as your own grandchild, for example. What this Everyman becomes afraid of is that he won't be allowed back in any form. As in the original version, none of his friends – his harlot, his cousins etc – are prepared to go with him to face Olodumare, though all are keen to inherit his wealth.

Towards the end (see Text 3) Everyman turns for help to Owo (Money), who he thinks of as his slave – but Owo scorns him for being a fool, and Everyman is destroyed. In the final scene, Everyman's daughter vows that her own child will not make the same mistake.

TEXT 3

NIGERIAN 'EVERYMAN' (extract 2)

EVERYMAN: Only an hour ago – I still had power
Over them all.
I commanded them – and they obeyed.
I bought them and I sold them as I pleased. Has Iku so quickly stripped me of my power? Am I already naked and deserted,
Even before my journey has begun?
Ha!
But Owo my most faithful servant
Shall not leave me now.
My friends and cousins have deserted me
But Owo shall be at my side.
Sule! Sule!

SERVANT: Yes master, I am here.

EVERYMAN: Go to the house and bring my money box. Bring me that great big heavy box
That's in my bedroom.
Bring it at once!

SULE *disappears and returns with several other servants carrying a large, heavy box. They place it centre stage.*

You may leave!

The servants retire.

I am afraid, Iku is near.
Sweat pours down my neck,
My belly is like water.
I cannot recognize myself.
Who am I? Am I not Everyman?
The rich man? The popular man?
Is this not my hand? Is this not my gown?
Is that not my money? My treasure?
Ah, Owo, do not desert me!

[continued over page]

He kneels down beside the box and prostrates to it.

    Stand you by me, my faithful servant.
    If you remain with me
    I'll fear no journey and no judgement,
    I'll bother not about Iku!

The lid of the box is thrown open, and OWO, *personified, jumps out. Owo is beautifully dressed in very rich cloth and holds a grinning mask in front of his face.*

OWO: Everyman, what's wrong with you?
    I see you getting hot and cold,
    Your dress is wet with sweat
    And butterflies are fluttering in your stomach.

EVERYMAN: But who are you?

OWO: So you don't know me by face?
    I am Owo your servant
    I am Owo your only friend in this world.

EVERYMAN: Owo, my friend,
    The sight of you gladdens my heart.
    No friend more loyal, no servant more faithful
    Did I have in this world.
    What I desired you bought –
    What I hated you destroyed.
    At my command, you would put any woman
    Into my bed and any man into jail.
    Your commander I was all these years,
    Now listen, for I shall command you
    For the last time.

OWO: Say what you need – I'll shun no work
    And no pain to supply your wants.

EVERYMAN: My problem is another one –
    I had a message…

OWO: A message? And from whom?

EVERYMAN: (*lowers his eyes, and speaks softly*): Yes, the messenger has come…

OWO: So sudden! Well, it's a surprise!

EVERYMAN: It's true – but you will follow me!

OWO: Follow you? That cannot be.

EVERYMAN: You are my property – do as you are told!

OWO: Your property! Ah, what a joke!

EVERYMAN: Will you revolt?
I'll show you back into your place! You, slave!

OWO *throws away the grinning mask. A fearful face (drawn in heavy make-up) appears underneath. He pushes* EVERYMAN *aside.*

OWO: I'll teach you who I am!
You dwarf!
How dare you think I am your slave?

EVERYMAN: Did I not command you at every hour?

OWO: Did I not rule in your heart and your soul?

EVERYMAN: Did you not serve me in the house and in the town?

OWO: Did I not fool you all your life?
How big, you felt yourself –
Owner of properties, owner of men.
You bought and sold, you commanded and ruled
Like a peacock you strutted around,
Who displays his feathers to his hens. Now you are naked and alone
Like a newly born swallow fallen from its nest.
Where are your friends, your harlots, now?
Was I your slave?
Well now: you'll make your trip,
Alone, a small and naked fool.
I'll stay right here – to play with other men.

He pushes EVERYMAN *down – and leaves.*

Obotunde Ijimere

C CREATIVE WRITING AND PERFORMING

The versions of **'Everyman'** we have looked at come from England in the sixteenth century, and Nigeria in the twentieth century, but several other versions have been written over the years.

1 Your writing task is to create a scene, based on one of the scenes you have been looking at, which is set in your own home country in the twenty-first century.

   Working either individually or in pairs, choose one of the following:
   - A scene featuring a speech by God – use whichever form of god you wish – which puts over his or her view of human behaviour. The speech should mention attitudes to money, along with anything else you think a god might wish to point out.
   - A scene involving a wealthy Everyman (or Everywoman) and a poor Neighbour, which shows us what kind of character Everyman is.
   - A scene in which Everyman/woman meets a 'money' figure – invent a suitable name – as in the 'Owo' scene you have been reading.
   - A scene where Everyman/woman arrives in heaven (or wherever) for the final judgement.

   Develop your choice in any way you wish. Change any of the names if you want to. Your version can be an adaptation of one of the scenes you have read, or a new idea of your own. Either way, use what you have read as a model for the form in which the script is written.

2 When you have finished a draft of your scene, try rehearsing it. Then make any changes or additions to the draft which you think would make the performance work better – adding more stage directions, for example.

Review

This unit has focused on a classic Middle English play, and a twentieth-century African adaptation. We have looked at traditional dramatic form and techniques, including the *personification* of abstract ideas. We have explored how *adaptations* are affected by different *cultural contexts* – but also what remains unchanged.

- As a class, make a list of things about the behaviour of 'everyman' which you would expect the character of God to criticise, if the play were rewritten today.
- Listen to a reading aloud of one of the scenes created during Activity C.

YEAR 9 UNIT 11

I remember

Aims

This unit focuses on some short examples of autobiographical writing, and on the interpretation of an author's perspective. Discussion and writing tasks include some creative writing and text analysis.

Starter session

Recall something that happened to you at least five years ago. Allow a minute's silence to revisit this memory. Then in pairs, recount your memory to your partner, using the past tense. Your partner should ask you two questions about what has been said.

A CREATIVE WRITING

1 As a class, read Margaret Atwood's prose piece called **'Autobiography'** (Text 1).

An *autobiography* is usually pretty lengthy: if you're telling the story of your life, then there's probably quite a bit to say. The text you have just read, though, is not an extract from a longer book, but a tiny recorded memory. Work through the following exercises, spending just a few minutes on each.

   a) Re-read the text, then try and record it in the form of a diagram – either a sketch, or a map. It needn't be a work of art – scribble labels on it if that helps.

   b) Compare your version with someone else's. Talk about any differences. Is one maybe more accurate than another?

2 Next, everyone in the whole class shuts their eyes for a couple of minutes and each person should travel backwards into their early memories. Which outdoor scene comes most clearly to mind? In your imagination, move around this place. Try turning round through 360 degrees and looking in each direction. Try walking away from the area, then looking back.

- Next, do a quick sketch or map of the place you were looking at in your own imagination.
- Compare sketches again. This time, talk your partner through what the sketch represents. They may be familiar with the place you've been thinking about, but the chances are you'll need to do some explaining and describing.

3 Now create your own piece of prose headed 'Autobiography'. Write about three paragraphs, around 150 words in total.

- One thing you could think about is tense. Will you use the past or the present tense, and what difference will that make? Could you use both? Take a look at the tenses in the Atwood text before you start.

TEXT 1

AUTOBIOGRAPHY

The first thing I can remember is a blue line. This was on the left, where the lake disappeared into the sky. At that point there was a white sand cliff, although you couldn't see it from where I was standing.

On the right the lake narrowed to a river and there was a dam and a covered bridge, some houses and a white church. In front there was a small rock island with a few trees on it. Along the shore there were large boulders and the sawed-off trunks of huge trees coming up through the water.

Behind is a house, a path running back into the forest, the entrance to another path which cannot be seen from where I was standing but was there anyway. At one spot this path was wider; oats fallen from the nosebags of loggers' horses during some distant winter had sprouted and grown. Hawks nested there.

Margaret Atwood

Vocabulary

loggers: lumberjacks; forestry workers

Context

Margaret Atwood

Margaret Atwood is widely admired both as a poet and a novelist. Her most celebrated novels include *Cat's Eye* and *The Handmaid's Tale*. She's a Canadian, and grew up in the rural 'bush country' of Northern Ontario and Quebec. **'Autobiography'** and **'Victory Burlesk'** are from a collection of very short prose pieces called *Murder in the Dark*, several of which record the author's childhood memories.

A EXTENSION

Actually, the **'Autobiography'** text printed on the left isn't quite complete. Margaret Atwood added a fourth and final paragraph (Text 2), which goes like this:

TEXT 2

> Once, on the rock island, there was the half-eaten carcass of a deer, which smelled like iron, like rust rubbed into your hands so that it mixes with sweat. This smell is the point at which the landscape dissolves, ceases to be a landscape and becomes something else.

1 What might this last sentence mean? Is there a point in your own piece of writing where the scene starts to 'dissolve', to 'become something else'?

2 Add one more paragraph to your own writing, which introduces a new object or person or event, and which begins to change the nature of that memory.
   - If there's nothing in your actual memory which you could use, you could invent something. Then you'll be moving, as writers often do, from autobiography into fiction.

B CRITICAL READING AND WRITING

1 Listen to a reading of Jean Rhys's story, **'I Used to Live Here Once'** (Text 3).

Like Margaret Atwood's **'Autobiography'**, this piece is based on a personal memory – in this case, of returning to the country, and to the house, where the writer had lived many years before. But **'I Used to Live Here Once'** is presented by the author as fiction – it appeared at the end of her final collection of short stories, published in 1976. Let's look at how it is composed.

2 In small groups, read the story through again aloud. Discuss each of the following questions, and jot down a short answer to each.
- One of the differences between Margaret Atwood's piece and this one is the shift from first to third person: 'I' becomes 'she'. What is the effect of this? Would this story come over differently if it were written in the first person?
- What is it, do you think, that makes the woman 'extraordinarily happy' (paragraph 2)?
- Does the story imply emotions other than happiness? What are they, would you say? At which points in the story do we sense these emotions? (Give a paragraph reference for each.)
- The final sentence – 'That was the first time she knew' – makes for a somewhat *enigmatic ending*. It leaves the reader to decide what it was the woman now knew, that she hadn't realised before. What do you think this was?

3 Using this discussion as a starting point, write a short account of this story, consisting of four paragraphs:
- Introduction and context
- How the writer develops our understanding of the situation
- How the story ends
- What the story makes you think about.

In the case of paragraphs 2 and 3, in particular, you will need to quote and refer to details from the text.

Vocabulary

pavé: alternative word for pavement, borrowed from the French
ajoupa: originally a Creole (West Indian) word for a tent or a hut

I USED TO LIVE HERE ONCE

para 1   She was standing by the river looking at the stepping stones and remembering each one. There was the round unsteady stone, the pointed one, the flat one in the middle – the safe stone where you could stand and look round. The next wasn't so safe for when the river was full the water flowed over it and even when it showed dry it was slippery. But after that it was easy and soon she was standing on the other side.

para 2   The road was much wider than it used to be but the work had been done carelessly. The felled trees had not been cleared away and the bushes looked trampled. Yet it was the same road and she walked along feeling extraordinarily happy.

para 3   It was a fine day, a blue day. The only thing was that the sky had a glassy look that she didn't remember. That was the only word she could think of. Glassy. She turned the corner, saw that what had been the old pavé had been taken up, and there too the road was much wider, but it had the same unfinished look.

para 4   She came to the worn stone steps that led up to the house and her heart began to beat. The screw pine was gone, so was the mock summer house called the ajoupa, but the clove tree was still there and at the top of the steps the rough lawn stretched away, just as she remembered it. She stopped and looked towards the house that had been added to and painted white. It was strange to see a car standing in front of it.

para 5   There were two children under the big mango tree, a boy and a little girl, and she waved to them and called 'Hello' but they didn't answer her or turn their heads. Very fair children, as Europeans born in the West Indies so often are: as if the white blood is asserting itself against all odds.

para 6   The grass was yellow in the hot sunlight as she walked towards them. When she was quite close she called again, shyly: 'Hello.' Then, 'I used to live here once,' she said.

para 7   Still they didn't answer. When she said for the third time 'Hello' she was quite near them. Her arms went out instinctively with the longing to touch them.

para 8   It was the boy who turned. His grey eyes looked straight into hers. His expression didn't change. He said: 'Hasn't it gone cold all of a sudden. D'you notice? Let's go in.' 'Yes let's,' said the girl.

para 9   Her arms fell to her sides as she watched them running across the grass to the house. That was the first time she knew.

Jean Rhys

Context

Jean Rhys

Jean Rhys is another major twentieth-century fiction writer. She is best known for her novel *The Wide Sargasso Sea*, written in the 1950s, but began writing short stories in the 1920s, and continued doing so into the 1970s. She was born on the French-Caribbean island of Dominica, but left there as a young woman to live in London, and later in Paris. In the 1930s she returned to her homeland as a visitor, but did not live there again. Several of her stories deal with the experience of Caribbean exiles, or – like this one – people who return.

C READING AND SPEAKING

Work in pairs.

1 Read through the poem **'Food. Music. Memory.'** (Text 4).

2 Talk about the way the poem is written. Decide who 'She' and 'I' are. Notice the ways the second verse repeats the first, and the ways in which it doesn't.

3 Then plan and rehearse a reading aloud, for two voices, which brings out what these words mean to the people who are saying them.

TEXT 4

FOOD. MUSIC. MEMORY.

She says: Cupcakes. Brownies. Pies. She says: Remember this. Bread. Stew. Sauce. She says: All that time. She says: Singing. All I taught you. She says: Crayon. Alligator. Boy Scouts. She says: Baseball. Soccer. Track. She says: I was there. Remember?

I say: Shouting. Silence. Shouting. I say: Remember this. Scotch. Vodka. Kahlua. I say: Cupcake. Meatloaf. Sauce. I say: Singing. All you would not tell me. I say: Crayon. Dancing. Guitar. I say: Belt. Hairbrush. Hand. I Say: I was there. Remember?

Susan Marie Scavo

Context

Susan Marie

Susan Marie Scavo lives in the USA. This poem appears in an anthology called *What Have You Lost* edited by Naomi Shihab Nye.

Vocabulary

Kahlua: alcoholic drink

TEXT 5

THE VICTORY BURLESK

I went to the Victory Burlesk twice, or maybe it was only once and one of my friends went the other time and told me about it. I enjoyed it both times. It was considered quite daring for young women to go to such a place, and we thought it was funny; it was almost as funny as church.

You got a stand-up comic, a movie and a man who sang or juggled plates, as well as the striptease act. They used a lot of coloured lighting, red and blue and purple. Each girl had a fake name: Miss Take, Miss Behave, Flame LeRew. I liked the names and the costumes, for their ingenuity, and I liked the more skillful girls, the ones who could twirl tassles or make their bellies or buttocks rotate in a circle. That was before they had to take it all off, there was an art to it, it was almost like the plate juggling. I liked the way they floated in the pools of coloured light, moving as if they were swimming, mermaids behind glass.

One woman began with her back to the audience, the spotlight on her. She was wearing long white gloves and a black evening gown with gauzy black sleeves that looked like membranous wings as she stretched out her arms. She did a lot with her arms and back; but when she finally turned around, she was old. Her face was powdered dead white, her mouth was a bright reddish purple, but she was old. I could feel shame washing through me, it was no longer funny, I didn't want this woman to take off her clothes, I didn't want to look. I felt that I, not the woman on the stage, was being exposed and humiliated. Surely they would jeer and yell things at her, surely they would feel they had been tricked.

The woman unzipped her black evening gown, slipping it down, and began to move her hips. She smiled with her white mask of a face and her purple mouth, inside her lips her teeth glinted, dull white pebbles, it was a mockery, she didn't intend it, she knew it, it was a trick of another kind but we didn't know who was playing it. The trick was that suddenly there was no trick: the body up there was actual, it was aging, it was not floating in the spotlight somewhere apart from us, like us it was caught in time.

The Victory Burlesk went dead. Nobody made a sound.

Margaret Atwood

Vocabulary

Burlesk: (or 'burlesque') a variety show (N. America)
membranous: thin and transparent, like a bat's wing

D CREATIVE WRITING

Work through the following on yopur own.

1 Read **'The Victory Burlesk'** (Text 5), another of Margaret Atwood's personal memory pieces, and think to yourself about why this memory stayed with her.

2 Then write a piece of your own, in which you recall in detail some experience that had a strong and memorable effect on you – moved you, or made you re-think things.
   - Try to describe things in a way that allows the reader to understand how you felt about the experience.

Review

This unit has looked at a group of texts about memories, both *autobiographical* and *fictional*. It has explored what these (sometimes *enigmatic*) memories mean to the writers, and some of the methods used to record them, such as uses of *tense* and *person*.

- As a class, talk about long-term memories, and what fixes them. What makes us remember a particular scene from a film or a novel, for example, when the rest of it has been forgotten?
- Listen to a reading aloud of one of the memories created during Activity A or D.

YEAR 9 UNIT 12

Migration

Aims

In this unit we'll be looking at a group of poems that deal with the experience of moving to a different country. The activities will also focus on some of the ways in which poets introduce and develop ideas.

Starter session

A silent start: in your mind recall the experience of entering a place that you hadn't been to before – maybe another country, or a town, or an unfamiliar building. Then decide on:

- Something about the place that attracted or excited you
- Something that made you feel 'out of place', a stranger, different.

Your teacher will ask some of you to volunteer to talk about these memories.

A READING AND SPEAKING

1. As a class, read Gillian Clarke's poem **'The Osprey'** (Text 1). Then agree on three facts about ospreys that we learn from this poem.

2. Now read the passage about the osprey from the ornithological guide (Text 2) produced by the RSPB (Royal Society for the Protection of Birds). What impression of ospreys does this passage give you?

3. What we are doing here, is comparing two different kinds of text. Think about what it is that makes them different.
   - If you re-formatted the RSPB passage in lines and verses, would it become a poem?
   - And if you re-formatted Gillian Clarke's poem as a prose paragraph, would it fit into an RSPB guidebook?
   - Why not…?

TEXT 1

THE OSPREY

Suddenly from the sea,
a migrating angel on its way
from Lapland to Africa
took a break at Cwmtydu.
It stayed three weeks,
like the moon roosting in an oak.

They fed it like a pet
on slithering buckets of silver
left over from the fish shop.
You could tell it was happy
by the way it splintered the sun
with its snowbird wings.

But its mind was on Africa,
the glittering oceans, the latitudes
sliding beneath its heart.
'Stay!' they said. 'Stay!'
But one day it lifted off and turned south
for the red desert, for the red sun.

Gillian Clarke

Gillian Clarke

Context

Gillian Clarke is a Welsh poet who writes in English. Her poetry for adult readers is widely admired, and popular in secondary schools. **'Osprey'** is from a book of poems for younger readers called *The Animal Wall*.

Vocabulary

Lapland: the far northern regions of Russia and Scandinavia

Cwymtydu: Welsh coastal village

One of the differences you may have come up with is the way poems tend to focus on *themes* or *ideas*. The various images combine in a way that gives them a meaning. In Gillian Clarke's poem, the osprey is on its way between two continents: winter is approaching, and it wants to be in Africa. It's a poem about 'migration'.

Migration is a word which we use both about birds and about human beings. 'Migrant' birds move from one continent to another as the seasons change. 'Emigrants' are people who leave the country where they were born; when they arrive elsewhere, they have become 'immigrants'.

4 Now read James Berry's poem, **'Black Kid in a New Place'** (Text 3), which expresses a child's experience of migration. You may need to talk through with your teacher what you think this poem is saying.

- What makes the kid stop feeling s/he is like a migrant bird?
- Why might s/he feel instead more like 'a sapling'?

TEXT 2

OSPREY

Pandion haliaetus (family Pandionidae) 51–58cm (20–23in) Easily distinguished from other large birds of prey by means of its contrasting dark brown upperparts and snow white underparts. **Flight** Long, somewhat narrow, wings having a distinct angle at the carpal joint. When fishing, flies at anything up to 30 metres (100 feet) above the water, hovering heavily before plunging after its prey. **Habitat** Lakes and rivers in wooded areas. **Distribution** Summer visitor with less than twenty pairs breeding in the Scottish Highlands after initial establishment at RSPB Loch Garten reserve; elsewhere on passage.

RSPB Guide to British Birds

Context

James Berry

The poet James Berry was born in 1924 in Jamaica, then moved to Britain shortly after the Second World War, a time when immigration was particularly encouraged. He has written several popular books for younger readers as well as poetry for adult readers. **'Black Kid in a New Place'** is taken from *When I Dance*.

TEXT 3

BLACK KID IN A NEW PLACE

I'm here, I see
I make a part of a little planet
here, with some of everybody now.

I stretch myself, I see
I'm like a migrant bird
who will not return from here.

I shake out colourful wings.
I set up a palmtree bluesky
here, where winter mists were.

Using what time tucked in me, I see
my body pops with dance.
Streets break out in carnival.

Rooms echo my voice. I see
I was not a migrant bird. I am
a transplanted sapling, here,
blossoming.

James Berry

Vocabulary

sapling: young tree

B SPEAKING AND CREATIVE WRITING

1 Working in groups, plan and rehearse a reading aloud of Grace Nichols' poem **'Out of Africa'** (Text 4).

- You will need to decide first what you think each line means. Check the Vocabulary notes where needed.
- Then you will need to decide on the *tone* in which each line should be spoken. Do the lines build up a particular impression of Africa, or the Caribbean, or England? Are there variations in tone?
- Finally you will need to decide how the lines can best be divided up between you.

2 Next, working individually, write an 'Out of / Into' poem of your own.

- If you have lived in two countries, or visited another country, write a verse about each, using the structure of Grace Nichols' poem as a model.
- Or you could write about travelling from the town that you live in, to another town that you know.
- In either case, concentrate on those things that are typical of each place, that – for you – give the place its character, or cultural style.

TEXT 4

OUT OF AFRICA

Out of Africa of the suckling
Out of Africa of the tired woman in earrings
Out of Africa of the black-foot leap
Out of Africa of the baobab, the suck-teeth
Out of Africa of the dry maw of hunger
Out of Africa of the first rains, the first mother.

Into the Caribbean of the staggeringly blue sea-eye
Into the Caribbean of the baleful tourist glare
Into the Caribbean of the hurricane
Into the Caribbean of the flame tree, the palm tree,
the ackee, the high smelling saltfish
and the happy creole so-called mentality.

Into England of the frost and the tea
Into England of the budgie and the strawberry
Into England of the trampled autumn tongues
Into England of the meagre funerals
Into England of the hand of the old woman
And the gent running behind someone
who's forgotten their umbrella, crying out,
'I say… I say-ay.'

Grace Nichols

Vocabulary

suckling: breastfeeding (or a child who is fed that way)

baobab: or 'monkeytree'; thought to be one of the most ancient types of tree on earth.

maw: old word for mouth

baleful: grim, hostile

ackee: a tropical fruit

creole: born in the West Indies

meagre: small, inexpensive

Context

Grace Nichols was born in Guyana, in the West Indies, where her family was originally of African descent. She moved to England in the 1970s, where she has lived and worked since. Many of her poems have dealt with the subject of moving between cultures and continents, both the history of the slave trade which abducted so many African people into the Americas, and the more contemporary experience of migration.

C READING FOR MEANING

The last two poems in this unit explore some of the feelings that migration can involve.

1 Look at the extract from **'The Arrival of Brighteye'** (Text 5), by Jean Binta Breeze. The speaker is a young girl who is living with her Granny in Jamaica, while awaiting a message from her mother, who has emigrated to London, to follow her across.

This prose-poem is written in Caribbean dialect, so can only be read in the accent it records. If there are no Caribbean voices in your class, try sharing the paragraphs out and reading the text as it is written, *phonetically*: the consonant 'th' becomes hardened to 'd', and various vowel sounds are also re-written. The form in which the words are written makes it clear how they should be said, and hearing the words will clarify the meaning. Practise first, then do a shared reading.

2 Now talk about how Brighteye's story might continue.
- What might she gain from the journey abroad?
- What might she lose?

3 Finally, read Imtiaz Dharker's poem **'Exile'** (Text 6). She too is a poet who has moved between countries – from Pakistan to India, via Scotland. What does this tiny poem say about that experience?

TEXT 5

THE ARRIVAL OF BRIGHTEYE (extract)

My mommy gone over de ocean
My mommy gone over de sea
she gawn dere to work for some money
an den she gawn sen back for me

one year
two year
tree year gawn

four year
five year
soon six year come

> Granny seh it don't matter
> but supposin I forget her
> Blinky Blinky, one two three
> Blinky, Blinky, remember me

Mommy sen dis dress fah ma seventh birthday. Ah born de day before chrismas, an she sen de shoes an de hat to match. Ah wear it dat very chrismas Sunday, an wen ah come out into de square, on de way to church wid Granny, all de ole man dem laughing and chanting

> Brighteye Brighteye
> red white an blue
> Brighteye Brighteye
> yuh pretty fi true

an Granny seh don't walk so boasy, mind ah don't buk up mi toe an fall down an tear up de dress pon rockstone, because she going to fold it up an wrap it up back in de crepe paper wid two camphor ball an put it back in de suitcase, dis very evening, as soon as ah tek it aff, put it back in de suitcase dat ah going to carry to Englan.

Crass de sea, girl, yuh going crass de sea, an a likkle water fall from Granny eye which mek er cross an she shake mi han aff er dress where ah was holding on to make sure dat ah don't fall down for de shoes hard to walk in on rockstone, an she wipe er eye wid er kerchief.

An ah looking up in Granny face, ah know Granny face good. She say is me an mi madda an grampa put all de lines in it, an ah wondering which lines is mine, an ah tinking how Granny face look wen sun shine an de flowers bloom, an wen rain full up de water barrel, an wen drought an de bean tree dead, an wen Grampa bus a rude joke, ah know Granny face but now she wipe er eye an lock up er face tight, an ah feel someting tight lack up in my troat, fah ah can't remember mi madda face, ah can't remember mi madda face at all.

[continued over page]

An all de time after dat, Granny finger in de silver thimble, flashing, sewing awn de red, white an blue lace she buy at market, sewing it awn to de church hat to mek pretty bonnet to go wid de dress. She say ah mus put awn de whole outfit when ah reach, so mi madda can see how ah pretty, an how she tek good care of mi, an she pack de cod liver oil pill dem in mi bag an say memba to tek one every day on de boat so mi skin would still shine when ah reach, an when we leaving de village in de mawning all de ole man dem singing

> Brighteye, Brighteye,
> going crass de sea
> Brighteye, Brighteye
> madda sen fi she
> Brighteye, Brighteye
> yuh gwine remember we?

Jean Binta Breeze

Vocabulary

boasy: proud (Afro-Caribbean)

camphor ball: or 'mothball'; traditional means of protecting clothing from insects etc

Context

Jean Binta Breeze

Jean Binta Breeze is a Caribbean poet and performer who has lived both in the West Indies and in Britain. **'The Arrival of Brighteye'**, a prose poem describing the experience of a young West Indian girl who follows her mother to England, was commissioned by the BBC as part of the *Windrush* series, which recalled West Indian emigration to England in the 1940s and 1950s.

TEXT 6

EXILE

A parrot knifes
through the sky's bright skin,
a sting of green.
It takes so little
to make the mind bleed
into another country,

a past that you agreed
to leave behind.

Imtiaz Dharker

Context

Imtiaz Dharker was born in Lahore (Pakistan), grew up in Glasgow (Scotland), and now lives in Bombay (India). She is both a poet and an artist: her books combine poems and drawings, and are published in the UK by Bloodaxe. **'Exile'** is from her first collection, *Purdah*, which explored the experience of moving between cultures.

Review

This unit has explored a group of poems about the experience of *migration*. We have looked at some of the ways poets develop *themes*, through the use of *figurative imagery*, for example, or the patterning of language.

- As a class, discuss what these poems tell us about the experience of moving between different countries, and different cultures.
- Listen to a reading aloud of one of the poems created during Activity B.

YEAR 9 UNIT 13

Weird tales

Aims

This unit looks at two traditional African stories involving unreal events. It explores the narrative structure of these stories, and how they might relate to the real world. The unit works towards the writing and performance of a 'weird tale'.

Starter session

In Britain, cockerels go *'cock-a-doodle-doo!'*. In France, they go *'cocorico!'*. In Spain, they go *'quiquiriqui!'*. Practise saying each word aloud. Which do you prefer?

What are the English words for the noises made by cats, dogs and sheep? Write the answers on the board. Are these really the sounds that these animals make? Can anyone do better? Now how about dinosaurs?

A READING AND DISCUSSION

As a class, listen to a reading of the traditional African story **'The Nature of the Beast'** (Text 1). Then we'll look at how it is structured, and how it works as a story.

1 *Beginning*
The first sentence of a story often includes the word 'once': think of 'There was once…' or 'Once upon a time'.

- What does this word suggest about the nature of the story which is to follow?
- How would it be different, for example, if a story started: 'Last Sunday I was…'

Something else that happens in the first sentence of this story is that an animal speaks. This too is a signal: it's going to be one of those stories where animals talk.

- What other stories like that come to mind? (Cartoons are one common source.)
- What sort of stories would you call them?

2 *Ending*
The ending of this story is craftily structured. I'd say it consists of four sentences.
- The first is: 'With that she released the heron and it flew away.' That sounds a bit like the end of a story, doesn't it?
- But then comes another sentence: 'But as it went, it gouged out one of her eyes.' (When I first read the story, that second sentence came as a shock – did anyone else find that?)
- The third sentence is a formal signing-off – 'That is all' – rather like saying 'The End'.
- The fourth sentence needs more thinking about: 'When you see water flowing uphill, it means that someone is repaying a kindness.' A statement like this is what we might call the *moral* of a story: what it tells us about the world, and human beings, and how they behave.
- So what is the moral of **'The Nature of the Beast'**?

3 *Middle or Development*
A good ending often encourages us to look back at how a story develops, and to be clearer about the pattern and the significance of what has happened.
- At which points does one person/creature show kindness to another?
- At which points does one person/creature show ungratefulness to another?
- Which of these were least expected?

A word which is often used for stories of this kind is *fable*. The word implies two things: that the story is *unreal* (often because it involves animals who talk), but also that it carries a *moral*, and so connects back to the real world in that way.

Context

This story comes from a collection of traditional *African Folk-Tales*, originally told by oral storytellers from around the African continent, which have been recorded or written down, then translated into English by an American editor, Roger Abrahams (who gave the story its title). Hausa is one of the most widespread languages of West and Central Africa.

THE NATURE OF THE BEAST

A farmer was once working on his land, when a snake came up to him and said he was being chased by a lot of men.

'You must hide me,' said the snake.

'Where can I hide you?' said the farmer.

'Just save my life,' said the snake, 'that's all I ask.'

The farmer couldn't think of anywhere to hide the snake, so he crouched down and allowed it to creep into his belly. When the pursuers came up, they said, 'Hey you, where's the snake we were after – it came your way.'

'I haven't seen it,' said the farmer.

When the men had gone, the farmer said to the snake, 'The coast's clear – you can come out now.'

'Not likely,' said the snake, 'I've found myself a home.'

The farmer's belly was now so puffed out that you would have thought he was a woman with child. He was about to set off for home when he saw a heron. He beckoned to it and told it in a whisper what had happened.

'Go and squat,' said the heron, 'and when you've done, don't get up – keep straining until I come.'

The farmer did as he was told and, after a time, the snake put its head out and began snapping at flies. As it did so, the heron darted forward and caught its head in his bill. Then he gradually pulled the rest of the snake out of the farmer's belly, and killed it.

The farmer got up and said to the heron, 'You have rid me of the snake, but now I want a potion to drink because he may have left some of his poison behind.'

'You must go and find six white fowls,' said the heron, 'and cook and eat them – that's the remedy.'

'Come to think of it,' said the farmer, 'you're a white fowl, so you'll do for a start.' So saying, he seized the heron, tied it up, and carried it off home. There he hung it up in his hut while he told his wife what had happened.

'I'm surprised at you,' said his wife. 'The bird does you a kindness, rids you of the evil in your belly, saves your life, in fact, and yet you catch it and talk of killing it.'

With that she released the heron and it flew away. But as it went, it gouged out one of her eyes.

That is all. When you see water flowing uphill, it means that someone is repaying a kindness.

Traditional Hausa (West Africa)

B READING AND DRAMA

The second 'weird tale' came originally from the Fipa tribe in east Africa. The version printed here has been re-written by a contemporary English poet and story-writer, Brian Patten.

1 Read through **'The Talking Skull'** (Text 2), and see what you make of it.
- Why might people invent and remember and re-tell a story like this?
- Would you call this one a *fable*? Does it have a *moral*, do you think – or not?

2 Working in a group of four or five, devise a performance of this story which mixes storytelling with drama. Re-tell the story in any way you like.
- Will your version have a *narrator*? More than one?
- What *tone* will the story be told in?
- How many characters?
- How will you present the skull? As a person? A cap? A football?
- How will you perform the skull's voice?

When the Fipa community tell each other stories, they traditionally begin like this:

> **Teller:** There was once a [hunter – or whoever the story is about]…
> **Listeners:** I was not there!
> **Teller:** There was once a [hunter]…
> **Listeners:** Tell me! Tell me!
> **Teller:** [There was once… & teller proceeds to tell story.]

If you wanted, you could start your performance in the same way.

THE TALKING SKULL

One morning while he was out stalking a deer a hunter tripped over a human skull hidden in the grass.

'Watch your step, fool!' it cried.

The hunter looked around, but saw nobody.

'I'm here at your feet,' said the skull.

The astonished hunter gingerly picked up the skull and examined it. For a skull to be imbued with such supernatural powers it must have met a very strange death, he reasoned.

'What killed you?' he asked.

'Talking killed me,' said the skull.

Now the hunter's tribe was ruled by a king who disliked the hunter intensely, and the hunter thought he could curry favour with the king if he presented him with such a remarkable object. So he put the skull in his hunting-bag and hurried back to his village.

The next morning before presenting himself to the king he checked that his imagination had not been playing tricks on him. He took the skull out of his bag and asked again, 'What killed you?' and again the skull replied, 'Talking killed me.'

Satisfied, the hunter approached the King.

'I've a remarkable gift for you,' he said.

'A gift? You? What can you offer a king?'

'A skull that talks, sire,' said the hunter.

'A talking skull? What kind of fool do you take me for?'

'I swear it's true, sire,' said the hunter. With a flourish and a great show of pomp he held up the skull and asked, 'What killed you?'

But this time the skull remained silent.

'Do not ridicule me,' said the King. 'Do not say another word.'

But the hunter would not listen. Again and again he asked, 'What killed you?' But the skull spoke not a word.

By now half the tribe had gathered round the hunter and the King, and the King felt belittled standing there giving the time of day to such a fool, a man who spoke to a skull and would not shut up even when ordered to do so.

'You've insulted me enough!' he roared, and he commanded the hunter to be dragged off to the forest and executed.

The hunter was beheaded and his head was thrown into the grass along with the skull that had been his downfall. The head provided a banquet for the ants and was picked clean within days.

It was only then that the first skull spoke again. 'What killed you, friend?' it asked the new skull lying beside it.

'Talking killed me,' said the second skull.

Traditional: Tanzania. Adapted by Brian Patten.

Context

This story appears in Brian Patten's absorbing book *The Story Giant*, in which four young people from around the world dream that they have arrived in the castle of a mysterious Giant, whose life has been dedicated to the collecting of stories. Patten's book contains dozens of traditional tales from around the globe: this one comes from the Fipa tribe, in the East African country of Tanzania.

C CREATIVE WRITING

1 The task here is to work in small groups to create a weird tale, or *fable*, of your own, similar in style to the ones you have read. It can either be a written story, or an oral tale.

If you decide to create the story orally, it will probably help to write down a skeleton plan on which the telling can be based.

Here are the requirements:
- The story has to have an *unreal* element: for example, some animal or object that speaks or sings.
- But it should also be about at least one ordinary human being.
- The story should be patterned: things are repeated, but with variations.
- It should end in an unexpected way.
- The story should carry some kind of *moral*: it should tell us something about human beings and how they behave, or how they ought to behave. This may take the form of a warning.

If you are stuck for a starting point, see if Posada's illustration for **'El Doctor'** (Picture 1) gives you any ideas…

Whether your story is written or oral, you may like to perform the final version to the rest of the class.

PICTURE 1

Context

José Guadalupe Posada

The Mexican artist and engraver José Guadalupe Posada (1852–1913) produced a huge range of illustrations for magazines, advertisements and other popular publications. He is best known for his skeletal figures. **'El Doctor'** was one of a series of printed folk stories for which Posada created the illustrations.

Review

This unit has looked at the tradition of *fables* – stories characterised by unreal or weird elements that also imply some kind of *moral*. We have also looked at the *development* of stories, and how they work towards an *ending*; and at the style in which stories are told.

- Are fables still a part of contemporary culture? As a class, can you think of any examples from books, songs, film, TV…?
- Listen to a reading or telling of one of the stories created during Activity C.

YEAR 9 UNIT 14

The one

Aims

This unit explores a group of texts about love relationships and marriage. The activities look at how these texts can be interpreted, in terms of personal feelings and cultural contexts.

Starter session

A says to B: Will you come out with me? As a class think of five different things B might say in response. The complication is that the five answers must start with the following five words: *Ah / Eh / I / Oh / Um*. Write the five answers on the board. Punctuate them carefully. Then perform them in whatever way you think each answer requires.

A READING AND DISCUSSION

1 In pairs, read **'I'm Really Very Fond'** (Text 1), and **'A Marriage'** (Text 2) – two short American poems about love relationships – and decide what you think each of these poems is saying about the relationship it refers to.
   - Decide which you think is the most significant single word in each poem.
   - Then decide on another word that helps you to understand the feelings involved – or two words, if you have different views.
   - Then explain your ideas to another pair.

2 Now read **'Song of the Bridesmaids'** (Text 3), a traditional African song/poem, and see how much you can deduce from the poem about the situation which the bridesmaids refer to.
   - How are marriages arranged in this culture, do you think?
   - What lifestyle do they lead to?
   - How does the bride feel about her future?

3 In pairs, write two diary entries by the bride, one just before and one some time after the marriage, based on what you have decided.

TEXT 1

I'M REALLY VERY FOND

I'm really very fond of you,
he said.

I don't like fond.
It sounds like something
you would tell a dog.

Give me love
or nothing.

But what I felt for him
was also warm, frisky,
moist-mouthed,
eager,
and could swim away

if forced to do so.

Alice Walker

TEXT 2

A MARRIAGE

Each week
he brought her
a rosebud.

Now
he sends
full roses
diamonds
furs.

She longs
for a bud
again.

Dudley Randall

TEXT 3

SONG OF THE BRIDESMAIDS

Oh beautiful bride, don't cry,
Your marriage will be happy.
Console yourself, your husband will be good.
And like your mother and your aunt,
You will have many children in your life:
Two children, three children, four …

Resign yourself, do like all others.
A man is not a leopard,
A husband is not a thunder-stroke,
Your mother was your father's wife;
It will not kill you to work.

It will not kill you to grind the grain,
Nor will it kill you to wash the pots.
Nobody dies from gathering firewood
Nor from washing clothes.

We did not do it to you,
We did not want to see you go;
We love you too much for that.
It's your beauty that did it,
Because you are so gorgeous…
Ah, we see you laugh beneath your tears!

Goodbye, your husband is here
And already you don't seem
To need our consolations…

Traditional: Rwandan (East Africa)

B READING FOR MEANING

The text for this activity is a scene taken from the middle of a play – Tanika Gupta's **'Skeleton'** – which is set in an Indian village in West Bengal. It's an intriguing play – but I'm not going to tell you anything about the characters, or about what has happened before this scene, or what will happen after. So reading it will be like turning on the TV half way through a drama series. You'll have to *infer and deduce* – or 'put two and two together.'

- Your chief source, since this is a playscript, will be the *dialogue*. How do the characters say their lines? What do they mean? Do you believe them?
- But Tanika Gupta is also one of those playwrights who provides lots of *stage directions* – movements, expressions, pauses – and these are often as important as the lines themselves. You might also give some thought to the *setting* of this scene: how does the river seem to fit into this story?

1 With these things in mind, work in pairs ('mixed' pairs if possible) and decide how much you can deduce about the following:
  - Anju and Gopal's past relationship
  - Anju and Gopal's present relationship
  - What kind of relationship you think the future may hold for them
  - In each case, jot down references to the things in the script which made you think this

2 Having talked about all this, you should be in a position to do a reading aloud of this scene – or even a performance, if you want to – which will bring out how you have interpreted it.

SKELETON: ACT 2 SCENE 6

Anju is squatting by the river. She is singing cheerfully and washing some clothes. She spreads out a couple of saris to allow them to dry in the sun and then she sits back and enjoys the peace. She seems happy. Gopal approaches the river and stands back watching her. Eventually, Anju becomes aware of him. When she sees him, she is uneasy but remains where she is. Gopal walks over to her and sits nearby.

GOPAL: You look well.
Anju looks at Gopal.
ANJU: You don't.
Gopal smiles.
GOPAL: Thanks! I haven't been sleeping well.
ANJU: Oh?
Gopal looks embarrassed. He looks at the river.
GOPAL: This river used to seem so vast, like an ocean ... remember? And now ... a stream.
Pause. Anju ignores him.
GOPAL: I'm sorry I didn't write.
ANJU: I'm sorry too.
There is an awkward silence.
ANJU: My father has bought my wedding sari and keeps asking when we are to be married.
Gopal is silent.
GOPAL: I need to finish my studies . . . if we marry now, we won't have anything to live on.
ANJU: That's not what you said last year.
GOPAL: Anju, things have changed, I've seen what real life is and ... We can't live on fresh air and love.
ANJU: You want me to wait another five years?
Gopal reaches over and tidies a strand of Anju's hair. Anju pushes his hand away.
GOPAL: Yes...
ANJU: And you're hoping I'll meet someone else in that time?
GOPAL: No.
ANJU: Coward.
Anju gathers up her clothes.

TEXT 5

GOPAL: Anju – please don't be angry with me.
ANJU: You've wasted my time.
GOPAL: Things have changed.
ANJU: What's changed? Your feelings?
Pause.
GOPAL: Yes. What do we have in common now? We live in different worlds.
ANJU: It's over?
GOPAL: Yes.
ANJU: I knew from the moment you stopped writing.
GOPAL: I didn't want to hurt you.
Anju laughs with sarcasm.
Anju sits down. Gopal squats down beside her. There is a moment's silence. They both watch the river, Anju dips her hand in.
ANJU: We tied our hands together with palm leaves and pretended we were married. How old were we?
GOPAL: *(laughs)* No more than ten ... Biju split a coconut for us ...
Anju starts to gather up her saris, etc. Gopal watches her.
GOPAL: Anju...
He stands up and then suddenly takes her in his arms and kisses her. Anju pushes him off... furious.
GOPAL: What are you doing?
GOPAL: I'm sorry... you just looked so beautiful.
ANJU: But you released me... remember?
Anju exits. Gopal sits and hangs his head.

Tanika Gupta

Context

Tanika Gupta is a contemporary British playwright from an Indian background. She has written dramas for radio and TV, and worked as a resident writer at the National Theatre. *Skeleton*, set in a village in Bengal, was the first of her plays to be staged, in 1997.

C   READING AND CREATIVE WRITING

1. As a class, look carefully at Gustav Klimt's painting **'The Kiss'** (Picture 1), painted at the beginning of the twentieth century, and talk about the style in which it has been created. Would you call it a *realistic* picture? Is it *abstract*? How is it different from a photograph? What *mood* does the painting create?

2. Can we deduce anything from the painting about the couple's relationship, in the way that we have done with the poems and the playscript in the previous activities?

   A writer who has tried to do just that is Lawrence Ferlinghetti. Listen to a reading of his poem **'Short Story on a Painting of Gustav Klimt'** (Text 5).

   Lawrence Ferlinghetti's poem *describes* in a precise way what is in the picture – but it also *interprets* what is going on.

3. As a class, talk about the phrases in the poem which add meanings to the picture.

   Of course, Lawrence Ferlinghetti knows no more than the rest of us what the story might be – all he has to go on is the painted image. And, in any case, deciding how one person feels about another is never easy. Has the poet got it right, do you think? Or not?

4. Write your own short story, or poem, or play scene, using Klimt's painting as a source of ideas. You could also draw on some of Lawrence Ferlinghetti's ideas, if you wish.

Context

Gustav Klimt

Gustav Klimt (1862–1918) lived in Vienna, and was one of the leading 'modernist' artists of his period. His work portrays human figures and relationships, but in a decorative, semi-abstract, style. **'The Kiss'** is one of his best-known works.

PICTURE 1

TEXT 6

SHORT STORY ON A PAINTING OF GUSTAV KLIMT

They are kneeling upright on a flowered bed
    He
              has just caught her there
                        and holds her still

        Her gown
              has slipped down
                        off her shoulder

He has an urgent hunger
        His dark head
              bends to hers
                  hungrily

And the woman the woman
    turns her tangerine lips from his
        one hand like the head of a dead swan
        draped down over
                his heavy neck
        the fingers
            strangely crimped
                tightly together

her other arm doubled up
        against her tight breast
    her hand a languid claw
            clutching his hand
    which would turn her mouth
                to his

her long dress made
    of multicolored blossoms
        quilted on gold
her Titian hair
    with blue stars in it
And his gold
    harlequin robe
        checkered with
            dark squares

    Gold garlands

                stream down over
                            her bare calves &
                                tensed feet
Nearby there must be
          a jeweled tree
                 with glass leaves aglitter
                      in the gold air
It must be
        morning
              in a faraway place somewhere
They
     are silent together
            as in a flowered field
        upon the summer couch
              which must be hers
And he holds her still
      so passionately
holds her head to his
           so gently so insistently
      to make her turn
              her lips to his
Her eyes are closed
       like folded petals
She
   will not open
      He
            is not the One

Lawrence Ferlinghetti

Context

Lawrence Ferlinghetti

Lawrence Ferlinghetti was born in New York in 1919, and since the 1960s has been one of the USA's best-known modernist poets. The style of the poem's layout, which is characteristic of Lawrence Ferlinghetti's work, gives an idea of how it should be read aloud. He is also a painter.

Review

This unit has looked at a selection of texts which focus on love relationships, and at the ways we can interpret them. We have *inferred* things about these relationships from *poetic images*, *visual images*, *dialogue* and *stage directions*.

- As a class, talk about the ways we try and deduce how one person feels about another, in literature or in life.
- Listen to a reading of one of the pieces created during Activity C.

YEAR 9 UNIT 15

Man Friday

Aims

This unit is based on short extracts from a classic eighteenth-century novel, and a twentieth-century play based on the same story. It explores differences in cultural perspectives that develop over time.

Starter session

Your teacher will divide your class in to groups of six to eight students. In each group, A becomes 'Master', and delivers an instruction to B. B asks a question about the task he/she has been given, which A answers. B then becomes Master, and passes the more detailed instruction on to C, who asks a further question about the task, and so on. When the final servant in the group has received the instruction, he/she becomes Master, and begins a different instruction, which is sent back in the same way.

A CREATIVE READING

1. Working together as a class, begin by reading the Context note for the extract from Daniel Defoe's novel **'Robinson Crusoe'** (Text 1). Then read the extract itself, in which Crusoe describes his meeting with the rescued Carib native, Man Friday.

2. It should be clear from this extract that the two characters are showing *positive attitudes* towards each other. Friday's attitude towards Crusoe is straightforward: Crusoe has just saved his life. What about Crusoe's attitude to Friday?

    - Working in pairs, make a list of *positive* words or phrases which Crusoe uses when writing about Friday – your list should include two examples from each of the extract's five paragraphs.

3. How would you define the relationship between the two characters? In particular, think about the question of status (i.e. 'social position in relation to others'.)

TEXT 1

ROBINSON CRUSOE
(Extract: Crusoe describes 'Man Friday')

He was a handsome fellow, with straight strong limbs, not too large; and as I reckon, about twenty-six years of age. He had a very good countenance; he seemed to have something very manly in his face, and yet he had all the sweetness and softness of a European in his countenance too, especially when he smiled. His hair was long and black, not curled like wool; his forehead very high and large, and a great vivacity and sparkling sharpness in his eyes. The colour of his skin was not quite black, but very tawny.

After he had slumbered about half an hour, he waked again, and came out of the cave to me; for I had been milking my goats, which I had in the enclosure just by. When he espy'd me, he came running to me, and laid his head flat upon the ground, close to my foot, setting my other foot upon his head; and after this, made all the signs to me of servitude and submission imaginable, to let me know how he would serve me as long as he lived. I let him know I was very well pleased with him; in a little time, I began to speak to him, and teach him to speak to me; and first, I made him know his name should be Friday, which was the day I saved his life; I likewise taught him to say Master, and then let him know, that was to be my name; I likewise taught him to say yes and no, and to know the meaning of them.

Never man had a more faithful, loving, sincere servant than Friday was to me; without passions, sullenness, or designs; his very affections were ty'd to me, like those of a child to a father; and I dare say he would have sacrificed his life for the saving of mine upon any occasion whatsoever; and the many testimonies he gave me of this soon convinced me that I needed to use no precautions as to my safety on his account.

I was delighted with him, and made it my business to teach him everything that was proper to make him useful, handy, and helpful. The next day I set him to work beating some corn out, and sifting it in the manner I used to, and he soon understood how to do it as well as I, especially after he had seen what the meaning of it was; for after that I let him see me make my bread, and bake it too, and in a little time Friday was able to do all the work for me, as well as I could do it myself.

[continued over page]

This was the pleasantest year of all the life I led in this place; Friday began to talk pretty well, and understand the names of almost everything I had occasion to call for, and of every place I had to send him to, and talked a great deal to me; so that, in short, I began now to have some use for my tongue again, which indeed I had very little occasion for before; beside the pleasures of talking to him, I had a singular satisfaction in the fellow himself; his simple honesty appeared to me more and more every day, and I began really to love the creature; and on his side, I believe he loved me more than he had loved anything before.

Daniel Defoe

Vocabulary

countenance: face
vivacity: liveliness
tawny: dark
espy: see (old word)
submission: giving in; obedience
sullenness: moodiness, bad temper
testimonies: evidence

Context

Daniel Defoe

Daniel Defoe (1659–1731) was one of the very earliest English novelists. For most of his life he worked as a journalist. *The Life and Adventures of Robinson Crusoe*, his first work of fiction, was published in 1719. It was an immediate popular success, and remains a key work in English literary history.

During the previous century, European merchants and military forces had been invading and colonising the coastal areas of North and South America, including the West Indies. The idea for Daniel Defoe's book came from a real-life event: following a shipwreck, a Scottish sailor called Alexander Selkirk had spent four years alone on an island in the Caribbean, before being picked up and returned.

When *Robinson Crusoe* was published, the author pretended that it was not a novel at all, but a factual, autobiographical account, written by a shipwrecked sailor; the book recorded in detail Crusoe's experience of living for twenty-eight years on an uninhabited Caribbean island, until he was finally rescued and brought back to England.

Daniel Defoe

In the twenty-fifth year of Crusoe's adventure, a tribe of cannibals visit the island, bringing with them a number of Carib prisoners, whom they begin to kill and eat. Crusoe explains how he attacked the cannibals with his musket, driving them from the island, and saving the life of one of the prisoners, whom he named 'Man Friday'.

In the extract printed here, Crusoe describes the beginning of his relationship with Friday, who becomes Crusoe's servant, and remains with him for the rest of his time upon the island. (The extract has been condensed.)

B DRAMA AND READING

1 In pairs, rehearse a performance of **Extract 1** from **'Man Friday'** (Text 2). Even if you are reading the script, try and include the actions as well as the words.

2 Now look again at the original extract from **'Robinson Crusoe'** (Text 1), on which this scene is based, and talk about the differences between the two.
   - What is the effect of the change from prose to dialogue?
   - Has the *tone* changed?
   - Has the characterisation altered?
   - What attitudes do the characters reveal?
   - Do the two writers have a different *perspective* on what is going on?

3 Lastly, as a class, read **Extract 2** from **'Man Friday'** (Text 3), in which the two characters discuss the issue of 'rights and responsibilities'.
   - What are 'rights'? What are 'responsibilities'?
   - What does this extract tell us about each of the two characters?

TEXT 2

MAN FRIDAY (Extract 1)

CRUSOE: You – Friday.

FRIDAY: Fri-day.

CRUSOE: Yes, good. Friday.

FRIDAY: (*nods*) Friday. (*Points to Crusoe.*) Friday?

CRUSOE: (*shakes head*) No. Me – (*Points to self.*) Me – Master.

FRIDAY: Me, Master.

CRUSOE: No, no, no. (*Points to self.*) Master. (*Points to Friday.*) Friday. (*Points to self.*) Master.

FRIDAY: Ah. (*Pointing rapidly from one to the other.*) Friday. Master. Friday. Master. Friday. Master.

CRUSOE: You're sharp, lad, you're sharp. Maybe it won't take too long to teach you English.
(*CRUSOE gets up, impatient to start. Points to his head.*)
Head. Head.
(*FRIDAY shakes his head in disbelief. CRUSOE nods emphatically. Pointing.*)
Head. Head.
(*FRIDAY grins, shakes his head.*)
(*Pointing.*) Head. Nose. Mouth. Hand. Arm. Body. Leg. Foot.
(*CRUSOE looks up from pointing to his foot.*)

FRIDAY: (*shakes his head, pointing to his head*): Baskra.
(*Points to his nose.*) Logglephan.
(*To his mouth.*) Omra.
(*To his hand.*) Lashti.
(*To his arm.*) Clyserta.
(*To his body.*) Olavara.
(*To his leg.*) Eegra.
(*To his foot.*) Dom.

CRUSOE: Friday!

FRIDAY: Master?

CRUSOE: (*jabbing a finger at Friday's head*) Head. Head.

FRIDAY: (*cautiously*) Baskra?

CRUSOE: No, not bloody baskra. Head. Head.
(*Touches his own head, then Friday's. CRUSOE raises his fist, then lowers it as FRIDAY crouches away.*)
This is my island, this is Master's Island and Master is an Englishman and so this island is a part of England and so we will talk English, English. Friday will talk English too. And you'll stop speaking that black language of yours if I have to tear your tongue out by the roots.
(*Pulls himself together.*)
Start again. (*Pointing.*) Friday.

FRIDAY: Friday.

CRUSOE: (*pointing*) Master.

FRIDAY: Master.

CRUSOE: (*pointing*): Head.

FRIDAY: Ba –
(*CRUSOE raises his fist.*)
Ed.

Adrian Mitchell

Context

Adrian Mitchell

Adrian Mitchell was born in London in 1932. In the 1950s he worked (like Daniel Defoe) as a journalist. Since the 1960s he has written a wide range of scripts for theatre and TV, as well as novels and poetry. He has always been a writer with political views: anti-war, anti-racist, anti-capitalist.

By the 1960s, the history of British Imperialism, which had led to Britain's dominance of so many parts of the world, and of so many different ethnic populations, had become an embarrassment to the many Britons who shared Mitchell's political views. For someone like Mitchell, a story such as *Robinson Crusoe*, in which the English sailor became the 'Master' of a Caribbean island, took on a new significance.

In 1972, Mitchell wrote a TV play called *Man Friday*, later adapting it for the stage (the extracts in this unit come from the stage version), and finally as a novel. The title of Adrian Mitchell's version is worth noting. He adjusts Daniel Defoe's story in various ways, but essentially it is told from the point of view of the servant, Man Friday.

TEXT 3

MAN FRIDAY (Extract 2)

(*CRUSOE sits in his corner, surrounded by his many possessions. He is reading a Bible. FRIDAY rings the ship's bell that hangs beside CRUSOE's door.*)

CRUSOE: Friend or foe?

FRIDAY: (*outside*) Friday, Master.

CRUSOE: Come in.
(*FRIDAY comes in. CRUSOE motions him to sit on the floor, FRIDAY sits.*)
You're back early this morning, Friday. Working fast today? Washed out all the pans? Lit the signal fire? Caught plenty of fish? Or were you going after the goats today?

FRIDAY: (*shaking his head*) I've been swimming.

CRUSOE: Good, good, trying to salvage some more treasure from that old wreck, eh?

FRIDAY: No, Master, I've been swimming because I like to swim. My body agrees with the ocean.

CRUSOE: But what about your duties, Friday? Your jobs? You know what I keep telling you. It's all very well to talk about your rights, all very well. But what about your responsibilities, eh?

FRIDAY: I am not doing responsibilities today, Master. I am doing rights.

CRUSOE: And what about the fish? What are we going to eat tonight?

FRIDAY: The fish tell me that they will come if Master calls them.

CRUSOE: Friday, it's your job to fish. And the signal fire, what about the signal fire?

FRIDAY: The signal fire says that Master may light it whenever he chooses.

CRUSOE: But, Friday, that's another of your little tasks.

FRIDAY: No, Master. It is Master's turn to work.

CRUSOE: You think I don't work? You accuse me of not working? How do you suppose we'd survive on this island if it wasn't for me?

FRIDAY: Friday fishes, Friday hunts, Friday lights the fires, Friday cooks, Friday mends the clothes –

CRUSOE: And he does all those things very well indeed. You have a good hunting eye and supple muscles, so you work with your eyes and with your body. But I am Master, and I work with my brain.

FRIDAY: Has your brain built a raft yet?

CRUSOE: I'm working it out. I'm working it out on paper.

FRIDAY: A raft of paper?

[continued over page]

CRUSOE: (*angry*) I'M WORKING IT OUT! Listen. Who has the burden of making all the decisions on this island? Who has to say when we shall eat and when we shall refrain from eating? Who is responsible for assigning tasks, for maintaining morale? Who decides, with the help of God Almighty, what is wrong and what is right?

FRIDAY: I would like to try to do that work, Master.

CRUSOE: No, no, Friday. That is Master's work.

FRIDAY: And so Friday is just one of Master's possessions. Like his sunshade. Like those slaves you told me about.

CRUSOE: That's unkind and ungrateful, Friday. I don't look on you as a slave.

FRIDAY: Then what am I?

CRUSOE: You are an ignorant savage.
(*Calming.*)
I'm just trying to teach you, Friday.

Adrian Mitchell

C   CRITICAL WRITING

The way we look at things depends a lot on our cultural background, the *context* in which we were brought up, and learned to think. Living in different countries, believing in different religions, or belonging to different generations, for example, are all bound to affect the way we see the world.

Although both Daniel Defoe and Adrian Mitchell are white English writers, they come from different periods of history, and so look at things in different ways: their *cultural perspectives* are not the same.

1 The final task in this unit is to write a short essay comparing the extracts from **'Robinson Crusoe'** and **'Man Friday'** which we have been studying. The notes and discussions from Activities A and B should help with this task. Here is a plan you could use if it fits your ideas:
- Paragraph 1. Write something about the context of each writer's work, drawing attention to differences.
- Paragraph 2. Describe the impression of the two characters – Crusoe and Friday – you get from the Defoe extract. Quote some words or phrases from the text.
- Paragraph 3. Describe the impression of the two characters and their relationship that you get from the Adrian Mitchell extracts. Quote some lines from the script.
- Paragraph 4. Say something about the difference between the ways in which the two works are written, and any effect this has.
- Paragraph 5. Explain why you think Adrian Mitchell decided to create his new version of the story, and what it leaves the reader thinking.

Review

This unit has looked at extracts from a classic eighteenth-century novel and a twentieth-century dramatisation. It has focused on differences in *cultural contexts*, and the changes in authors' *values* and *perspectives* which that can produce. The unit has also looked at differences in *tone*, and differences in *characterisation*, including characters' *attitudes*.

- As a class, discuss the implications of giving an adaptation of *Robinson Crusoe* the title *Man Friday*.
- Listen to one of the performances created during Activity B.

Acknowledgments

The publishers would like to thank the following for permission to use copyright material. Every effort has been made to trace copyright holders and to obtain their permission for the use of copyright material. The author and publishers will gladly receive information enabling them to rectify any error or omission in subsequent editions.

Pictures:
'Automat' by Edward Hopper, courtesy of Des Moines Art Center
'Sunlight in a Cafeteria' by Edward Hopper, courtesy of Yale University Art Gallery, New Haven
'Bilingual Dog' by Jose Garcia Cordero, courtesy of Thames & Hudson and the artist
'El Doctor' by Jose Guadalupe, courtesy of the artist
'The Kiss' by Gustav Klimt, courtesy of The Bridgeman Art Library

Text:
JOHN AGARD: from 'Anancy's Thoughts on Colours' from *Weblines* (Bloodaxe Books, 2000), by permission of John Agard c/o Caroline Sheldon Literary Agency; MARGARET ATWOOD: 'Autobiography' from *Murder in the Dark* (Jonathan Cape, 1984); JAMES BERRY: 'Bye now' and 'Black Kid in a New Place' from *When I Dance* (Hamish Hamilton, 1988), by permission of the author; JEAN 'BINTA' BREEZE: from *The Arrival of Brighteye* (Bloodaxe Books, 2000), by permission of the publisher; KEN CAMPBELL: from *Skungpoomery* (Methuen Publishing, 1976), by permission of the publisher; GILLIAN CLARKE: 'The Osprey' and 'Chip-hog' from *The Animal Wall* (Pont/Gomer Press, 1999); DOMINIC COOKE: from *Arabian Nights* (Nick Hern Books, 1998), by permission of the publishers; IMTIAZ DHARKER: 'Exile' from *Postcards from God* (Bloodaxe Books, 1997), by permission of the publisher; TANIKA GUPTA: from *Skeleton* (Faber & Faber, 1997); GRACE HALLWORTH: 'Shiner' from *Mouth Open, Story Jump Out* (Methuen Books, 1984), © 1984 by the author, by permission of Marilyn Malin Representation; OBOTUNDE IJIMERE: from 'Everyman' in *The Imprisonment of Obtalo & Other Plays* (Heinemann, 1966), by permission of Reed Publishers, Oxford; JACKIE KAY: 'Old Tongue' from *Hello New*, edited by John Agard (Orchard Books, 2000), by permission of the author; JAMAICA KINCAID: 'Girl' from *At the Bottom of the River* (Pan/Picador, 1984), by permission of Macmillan Publishers Ltd; ADRIAN MITCHELL: from 'Man Friday' in *Man Friday & Mind Your Head* (Eyre Methuen, 1974); GRACE NICHOLS: 'Out of Africa' from *Lazy Thoughts of a Lazy Woman* (Virago Press, 1989), © Grace Nichols, and 'Red' from *Sunrise* (Virago Press, 1996), © Grace Nichols, by permission of Curtis Brown Ltd., London, on behalf of Grace Nichols; JEAN RHYS: 'I used to live here once' from *Sleep It Off Lady* (Andre Deutsch, 1976), by permission of Penguin UK; SISTA ROOTS: 'Dictionary Black' from *Watchers and Seekers*: O*riginal Anthology of Creative Writing by Black Women Living in Britain*, edited by Rhonda Cobham and Merle Collins (The Women's Press, 1987); SUSAN MARIE SCAVO: 'Food Music Memory' from *What Have You Lost?*, edited by Naomi Shihab Nye (HarperCollins Publishers Inc.,1999); TRADITIONAL: "Talk" (Ashanti) from *African Voices*, edited by Peggy Rutherford (Vanguard Press); 'Baby is a European' (Ewe Togo) from *African Poetry*, edited by Ulli Beier (Cambridge University Press); 'Locust' (Madagascar) from *The Unwritten Song*, edited by W. Trask (Macmillan); 'Song of the Bridesmaids' (Rwanda) from *African Poems & Lovesongs*, edited by C. & W. Leslau (Peter Pauper Press), © Peter Pauper Press, by permission of the publisher; ABDOURAHMAN WABERI: 'Nomadic Poem', translated by Veronique Tadjo, from *Talking Drums*, edited by Veronique Tadjo (A & C Black, 2000), by permission of the publisher; DEREK WALCOTT: from 'Pantomime' in *Remembrance & Pantomime* (Farrar, Straus & Giroux, 1980); BENJAMIN ZEPHANIAH: 'White Comedy' from *Propa Propaganda* (Bloodaxe Books, 1996), by permission of the publisher; 'Greet Tings' from *Talking Turkeys* (Viking, 1984), © Benjamin Zephaniah, 1994, by permission of the publisher; 'The British' from *Wicked World* (Puffin Books, 2000), text © Benjamin Zephaniah, 2000, by permission of the publisher.

Published by Letts Educational
The Chiswick Centre
414 Chiswick High Road
London W4 5TF

📞 020 89963333
📠 020 87428390
✉ mail@lettsed.co.uk
🌐 www.letts-education.com

Letts Educational Limited is a division of Granada Learning Limited, part of Granada plc.

© Nick jones 2002

First published 2002

ISBN 184085 7099

The author asserts the moral right to be identified as the author of this work.

All rights reserved. No part of this publication may be reproduced, stored in a retrieval system, or transmitted in any form or by any means, electronic, mechanical, photocopying, recording or otherwise, without either the prior permission of the Publisher or a licence permitting restricted copying in the United Kingdom issued by the Copyright Licensing Agency Ltd, 90 Tottenham Court Road, London W1P 9HE. This book is sold subject to the condition that it shall not by way of trade or otherwise be lent, hired out or otherwise circulated without the publisher's prior consent.

British Library Cataloguing in Publication Data
A catalogue record for this book is available from the British Library.

Developed and packaged by McLean Press Ltd

Commissioned by Helen Clark

Project management by Vicky Butt

Edited by Debbie Seymour

Cover design by bigtop, Bicester, UK

Internal design by bigtop, Bicester, UK

Production by PDQ

Printed and bound in the UK by Ashford Colour Press